VEGETARIAN MEDITERRANEAN COOKBOOK

SANAA ABOUREZK

VEGETARIAN MEDITERRANEAN COOKBOOK

125+ SIMPLE, HEALTHY RECIPES FOR LIVING WELL

ROCKRIDGE PRESS

For general information on our other products and services or to obtain technical support, please contact our Customer Care Department within the United States at (866) 744-2665, or outside the United States at (510) 253-0500.

Rockridge Press publishes its books in a variety of electronic and print formats. Some content that appears in print may not be available in electronic books, and vice versa.

Interior & Cover Designer: Patricia Fabricant
Art Producer: Michael Hardgrove
Editor: Gleni Bartels
Production Editor: Matthew Burnett

Photography © 2019 Annie Martin. Food styling by Chris Chapman, cover, and pp. ii, vi, viii, xiv, 8, 30, 54, 85, 90, 122, 138, 156; Stocksy/Miquel Llonch, p. xiii; Shutterstock/Foxys Forest Manufacture, p. 73; Shutterstock/Oliver Wilde, p 99.

Author photo courtesy of © Studio Blu.

ISBN: Print 978-1-64611-394-1 | eBook 978-1-64611-395-8

R0

TO MY SITO,
MY FIRST INSPIRATION
FOR COOKING.

AND TO MY DAUGHTER,
ALYA, YOUR LOVE KEEPS
ME GOING.

CONTENTS

INTRODUCTION

I was born and raised in Damascus, Syria. Each day, I woke up to street peddlers singing about the fruits and vegetables they were selling. My mother and our neighbors would run onto their balconies and yell and bargain with the peddlers for good prices. Each woman would lower a basket with money down to the peddler, who would exchange it for the produce. After lifting the basket up to the balcony, my mother would carefully evaluate each piece before deciding what to make for lunch. I loved the sounds of these peddlers, the smell of the fresh vegetables and herbs, and the aroma of a freshly cooked lunch.

During the summers, my family and I would go to our summer home, an olive farm in a village near the Mediterranean Sea. It was these fond childhood memories that inspired me to pursue food as a profession. I earned a bachelor's degree in agricultural engineering, followed by a master's degree in food nutrition. I would later travel to France and Italy for culinary school to educate myself further on Mediterranean cuisine.

Most farms in the Mediterranean region are relatively small. The farmer uses the land to grow enough vegetables for three to four families, and a few cows are raised for the family's milk, cheese, and butter—not meat. As such, families developed and passed down delicious recipes using only fresh ingredients from their farms: vegetables, grains, nuts, and dairy. It is for this reason most Mediterranean meals are vegetarian, or can easily lend themselves to be meat free. The recipes use what families had access to in the past, and they have stood the test of time because they're delicious!

The Mediterranean region is expansive and includes many countries and cultures. The cuisine certainly differs from country to country, but it also differs within each country. In the villages, tables are set with simple fare that revolves around the produce picked from local farms (perhaps the truest form of farm to table!), whereas food in larger cities is often more elaborate and tailored to impress tourists. But no matter where you go in the Mediterranean, the food is characterized by fresh ingredients that celebrate each region's best bounty.

In this book, I include recipes that focus on wonderfully flavorful and satisfying dishes that will have you feeling like you're in the South of France or on a Greek isle—all from the comfort of your own home.

FOUNDATIONAL FOODS AND FLAVORS

Mediterranean cuisine is famous for the freshness of its ingredients and intensity of flavors. From mouthwatering Italian pasta dishes crafted with the freshest tomatoes to appetizer plates in Spain containing the juiciest, most flavorful olives to pita bread served hot from the oven in Lebanon, each region's unique characteristics contribute to its cuisine and culinary offerings. Although each region has its own specialties, a few key ingredients have shaped the flavor profile we think of when we think of the Mediterranean.

Olive Oil

The Mediterranean landscape is abundant with beautiful olive trees that are so old they have become engrained within the regional heritage. For this reason, olive oil is the main fat used in most regional cooking. Its liberal use might inflate the calorie counts of some recipes, but olive oil is high in monounsaturated fat, a vital fat, and is extremely low in saturated fat, the fat we should avoid. Studies from such publications as the *New England Journal of Medicine* and *The American Journal of Clinical Nutrition* suggest that olive oil contains a compound essential to the health of our cells. Beyond its many health benefits, olive oil is simply delicious! Be sure to read Olive Oil 101 (page 72) for more information on this essential Mediterranean ingredient.

Onion

Another key ingredient for many Mediterranean recipes is the humble onion. Onions are inexpensive, can be stored for a long time, and their aroma while cooking will make anyone hungry. I recommend keeping a healthy stock of yellow onions for cooking, as well as sweet onions for salads. Onions are low in calories but high in antioxidants. They also are shown to lower blood cholesterol and regulate blood sugar. If you are prone to watery eyes while chopping onions, refrigerate them for 1 hour before cutting to lessen these effects.

Garlic

Garlic is used in most Mediterranean dishes and sauces. Garlic is a powerful ingredient believed to reduce blood pressure, control cholesterol, and protect against many forms of cancer. Almost every Mediterranean kitchen has at least one long garlic braid hanging on a shady wall or in a pantry closet, as the garlic stays fresher longer if kept out of direct sunlight. Garlic is commonly used in sauces, such as pesto and tomato sauce, or in dips and spreads, like hummus and aioli.

Herbs

Whether fresh or dried, herbs are essential to every dish produced in the Mediterranean. From chopped fresh parsley in tabbouleh salad to a fragrant basil pesto or the refreshing taste of mint added to a creamy yogurt dip, herbs often impart that *je ne sais quoi* to many regional specialties and provide a bright pop of color. Herbs also add many important vitamins and minerals to a dish without contributing any calorie-heavy carbs or fats.

Certain herbs are more widely used in some countries than others. Take, for instance, that the simple mix of dried basil, marjoram, oregano, and thyme is considered "Italian seasoning." But all countries throughout the region make liberal and regular use of herbs. See page 6 for some tips to prolong the life of your fresh herbs.

Cheese

Think of your favorite cheese from the Mediterranean region. Now ask your neighbor, significant other, or friend to do the same. Chances are, your choice may be a completely different one. As with many dishes, each country around the Mediterranean Sea has developed its own cheese and associated serving methods.

Greece is known for its feta, a soft, salty, crumbly cheese made from sheep, goat, or cow's milk. In Spain, you can find Manchego, an intense, zesty yet rich cheese, which is delicious when paired with jam. Visiting Turkey will lead you to kasseri, a soft, stringy cheese typically served for breakfast with sweet black tea. In Italy, popular cheeses vary by region. Mozzarella is a southern Italian specialty. Parmigiano-Reggiano, on the other hand, originates from Parma in the north, and makes the perfect accompaniment to nearly any pasta dish. France, too, has regional varieties of cheeses, with such offerings as Brie, Roquefort, and Comté.

Grains

In Eastern Mediterranean countries, such as Israel and Lebanon, wheat is plentiful. Here, locals make the tastiest flatbread and use bulgur wheat cereal as a main component in their cooking. Their dishes are simple, mostly salads with a grain base, and served with pita bread.

In the Southern Mediterranean, due to the vast, dry stretches of land and influence of their African neighbors, cuisine revolves mostly around stews, like the famous Moroccan couscous, which combines meat, vegetables, and, sometimes, fruit.

In the Northern Mediterranean region, Spain, France, and Italy are rich with more space and fertile lands. In addition to grains used for pastas, breads, and salads, the added influence of their European neighbors to the north constitutes a cuisine with more meat dishes than the rest of the Mediterranean, as well as the use of more cream and buttery sauces.

THE MEDITERRANEAN LIFESTYLE

The popular "Mediterranean diet" is not really a diet per se but, rather, a lifestyle. It is a way of life built around the freshness of the ingredients and pleasure of eating food that's good for you and tastes good, too.

Ingredients are picked fresh: produce from the farmers' market, bread from the neighborhood baker, and herbs from the pot on the kitchen windowsill. The recipes are simple and quick. Mealtime is an occasion, accompanied by close family and friends.

The biggest meal of the day is typically lunch, usually eaten after the workday, around late afternoon. Most people then take a short nap before going for a walk either through their village or the city's downtown. Dinner is a light affair, possibly as simple as cheese and crackers—something Americans would most likely consider a snack—before walking back home and heading to bed. These daily walks, before and after dinner, not only justify one's daily calories but also relax your digestive muscles and, in turn, help you sleep better!

Mediterranean people prefer a lively social setting: people talking and laughing and children playing. Socialization is a key part of mental health. Dining out in the Mediterranean follows suit. When you go to any restaurant, the table is yours not just for the hour but for the evening. You are encouraged to stay as long as you like, through drinks, appetizers, main dishes, and dessert, savoring each bite and great conversation with friends.

No one is checking their watch, and no one is checking their calories! The Mediterranean lifestyle, with all its walking and fresh, simple ingredients, allows people to maintain a healthy weight and way of life effortlessly.

CHAPTER 1
THE MEDITERRANEAN KITCHEN

Attempting unfamiliar recipes with unfamiliar ingredients can seem overwhelming. In this chapter I'll talk about the ingredients you'll need to harness the flavors of the Mediterranean to craft simple, satisfying dishes. I'll also give you some ideas on how to get started with the recipes.

THE PANTRY

While I was growing up, the inside of my grandparents' kitchen was full of myriad ingredients. The shelves were lined with small jars of jams, different varieties of olives, and spices galore. For the sake of your sanity and budget, in these recipes I'll stick to essentials of Mediterranean cuisine that can be found in most grocery stores within the United States. Following is a bit more detail on some things you should keep on hand.

Fresh and Perishable

Eggplant: Eggplants are a staple in vegetarian cooking because of their meaty texture and abundance of nutrients. In the Mediterranean they are used in main dishes like Eggplant Moussaka (page 86) and in dips and sides including classic baba ghanuj. For more information on picking an eggplant, see the recipe for Eggplant Parmesan (page 88).

Lemon: Almost all houses in the Mediterranean countryside have at least a couple lemon trees growing in the garden, which means the freshest fruit is easily accessible for cooking. The bright acidity of fresh lemon juice is a favorite addition to most salads and, I would go so far as to say, lemon zest is the best flavor enhancer for any dish.

Potato: Potatoes were brought from the New World to the Mediterranean region by the Spanish following the conquest of the Inca Empire, and within a few years of its introduction, the potato replaced the turnip as a major food source. Their starchy goodness adds heft to any dish and makes the perfect base for showcasing many different flavors.

Tomato: No Mediterranean household could survive without tomatoes. From tomato paste to sun-dried tomatoes, they're used in everything from sauces to stews for their color and acidic flavor. To pick a ripe tomato, smell near its stem—the more pungent the aroma, the better it will taste.

Zucchini: Zucchini is an incredibly versatile heart-healthy vegetable; you can marinate it for an appetizer (page 18), stuff some for a main dish (page 60), and dice them to add flavor and texture to soups, stews, and pilafs. I prefer small- to medium-size zucchini, about 6 inches long. When shopping, look for zucchini that feel heavy for their size and have smooth skin.

Spices, Nuts, and Seeds

Coriander: Coriander is the seed of the cilantro plant. Although coriander and cilantro come from the same plant, the seeds and leaves taste totally different from each other. One can still replace the other in recipes, though.

Cumin: Cumin is the spice used to a lend distinct smoky taste to hummus and bean soups, which is helpful because it is also believed to ease the beans' gas effect on our digestive system.

Turmeric: Ground turmeric is routinely added to mustard blends and relishes. It has anti-inflammatory properties and a mild flavor. The spice frequently lends its beautiful yellow color to rice dishes.

Nuts: Nuts, such as almonds, pistachios, and walnuts, are key ingredients in many Mediterranean dishes—from dinner to dessert. They add texture, flavor, and nutrients.

Sesame seeds: While tiny in size, sesame seeds have a large impact on Mediterranean cuisine. They can be used in desserts, are an ingredient in za'atar, and are the source of tahini's unique taste.

GET THE MOST OUT OF THE GROCERY STORE

Don't shop on an empty stomach. My most important tip for food shopping is to never head to the grocery store hungry. When you're hungry, everything looks tempting, and before you know it, you have a cart full of food you won't actually eat. Eat something first, review the dishes you are planning to cook for the week, make a list of things to buy, and stick to it!

Purchase seasonal fruit and vegetables. When something is in season, it's more flavorful. Check out your local farmers' market to see what's available. Because these items haven't traveled far, they'll be fresher—plus you'll be supporting local farmers. If you're not near a farmers' market, take a look at fruitsandveggies.org to see what's in season at your grocery store.

Use the smell and weight tests. Some fruits and vegetables *look* marvelous but don't *taste* marvelous. To find the good ones, bring the item close to your nose and take a big whiff. If it smells good, it most likely tastes good, too. Fruits and vegetables should also be firm to the touch and heavy for their size.

Avoid buying precut vegetables or fruit. It might save you time, but produce begins decaying and losing nutrients the second it's cut. It's also likely to cost more if someone has already cut it for you.

Do not wash the fruit or vegetables before you store them. Wash the vegetables and the fruit only when you plan to use them—this elongates their shelf life. Remember, too, not all fruits and veggies should be stored the same way. (I firmly believe refrigerating tomatoes kills their flavor, though this is a hotly debated topic.)

Canned and Bottled Goods

Beans: Canned black beans, chickpeas, and kidney beans are staples in every household. I've also listed them in the dry goods section, but their canned counterparts are great to use when you're short on time. Check the label and buy reduced-sodium varieties, and rinse them well before using to cut down on sodium intake.

Olive oil: As mentioned already, olive oil is a staple in Mediterranean cuisine. It's used in salad dressings, drizzled over cheese—you name it!

Tomato paste: Tomato paste is just concentrated tomatoes. It is used to thicken, color, and enrich the flavor of tomato sauces and stews.

Vinegar: Different vinegars are used for marinades, salads, and pickling. Keep white vinegar for pickling, red wine vinegar for marinades, and both red wine vinegar and balsamic vinegar for salad dressings and dips.

Dry Goods

Beans: Dried beans are a very inexpensive protein, and unlike canned beans, you can store them for a much longer time. I always stock my pantry with dried chickpeas, kidney beans, lima beans, and cannellini beans. See page 99 for information on batch cooking beans in a slow cooker.

Grains: Grains anchor many dishes in this book. I like to keep short-grain rice for stuffing vegetables, Arborio rice to make risotto, basmati rice for pilafs, and bulgur for tabbouleh. One of the greatest benefits of grains is the long-term storage potential. I like to shop for my grains in bulk at local co-ops and international food stores. Buying in bulk is more economical, and I don't lose any sleep over the ingredients going to waste due to their long shelf life.

Lentils: Whether black, brown, green, or red, lentils are an easy legume to cook. They do not require hours of soaking and cooking and they lend a nutrient-dense protein to your meal. For more information on lentils, see page 109.

Pasta: There are about 350 different types of pasta in the world, but I keep only a few of them in my pantry. I keep a short pasta like penne or orecchiette, a noodle pasta like spaghetti or angel hair, and a sheet pasta like lasagna.

HOW TO USE THIS BOOK

The recipes in this book are ones I love to cook both at home and in my restaurant. They originate from or are influenced by the countries surrounding the Mediterranean Sea—from Spain to Syria and everywhere in between. I've made them for friends and family and customers, all to rave reviews. Most are simple and easy to make, but there are a few that take a bit more time and will test your culinary skills. (Trust me, though—they're worth it!)

I try to use ingredients readily available at any American grocery store. I even put my ingredient lists to the test at my local supermarket in Sioux Falls, South Dakota. To my delight, I was able to find nearly everything necessary for this book; if I can find it in South Dakota, you can find likely it anywhere!

There are a few special ethnic ingredients included in some recipes that I thought were necessary for the authenticity of the dish. Although these ingredients can be ordered online easily, I provide tips for easy-to-find alternatives, when possible, so you won't have to take any extra steps before cooking.

You might be looking at this book and thinking to yourself, "Where do I begin?" My advice is to go through the pages and pick one or two intriguing recipes from each chapter. If you are a complete beginner to Mediterranean food, start by making a meal of Hummus (page 10), Greek Salad (page 49), and Fresh Sauce Pasta (page 124), with Red Wine–Poached Pears (page 158) for dessert. However, if you know your way around a kitchen, try Filo-Wrapped Brie with Orange Marmalade (page 26), Eggplant Moussaka (page 86), and Many Vegetable Couscous (page 105). Once you feel comfortable with a recipe, get creative with it! Recipes like Jeweled Rice (page 101) and Mushroom Pastilla (page 89) feature variation tips to add new flavors to the mix.

Each recipe includes labels for different lifestyles, diets, and schedules, so you can pick the best fit for you and your family. They also feature tips to help you get the most out of each recipe. These can range from ways to make prep easier to the best way to store leftovers or how to prepare a dish in advance.

ELEVATE YOUR INGREDIENTS

I am always intrigued when I order a vegetarian meal on a transatlantic flight. It usually consists of an iceberg lettuce salad with a single cherry tomato to start, mushy steamed vegetables with rice for a main, and a nice cup of Jell-O for dessert. When did vegetarianism become synonymous with having no teeth or the inability to chew? Vegetarian meals don't have to be sad and flavorless. Following are some ways to take your vegetarian dishes to the next level.

Add texture. I am a big fan of texture in any meal I cook—to me, it is an important element in every dish—from pilaf to a bowl of ice cream. Texture allows you to chew more, bringing out and enhancing the flavors in each bite. Next time you make a salad or stew, add sliced almonds or pine nuts or walnut pieces for added flavor and, more importantly, crunch.

Don't overcook. It is extremely important not to overcook your vegetables, which results in a loss of nutrients, flavor, and texture. Be aware of each vegetable's specific cooking time. For example, carrots and potatoes take longer to cook than zucchini or peas. An easy rule of thumb is to cook vegetables until they still have crunch but can be easily pierced with a fork.

Freeze your herbs. When buying fresh herbs, don't just remove a few leaves and put the rest in the refrigerator, unless you plan to use it within the next few days. Instead, chop the herbs, purée them with a little olive oil, and spoon the mixture into an ice cube tray. After a few days, transfer the frozen cubes into an airtight container and store them for up to 3 months. Anytime a recipe calls for fresh herbs, instead of running to the grocery store, reach into the freezer. In my freezer, I keep puréed basil, sage, thyme, and rosemary, along with a few other herbs just waiting to be used!

Infuse your oils. Herbs and spices can enhance the flavors of any dish. To infuse olive oil with an herby flavor, add your favorite herb or spice, like rosemary, mint, or black peppercorns to a clean glass jar or container. Slowly pour olive oil over the herb or spice. Cover the jar and let it rest in a cool place for about 1 week. When the flavor is strong enough for you, strain out the herb and rebottle the oil in a clean bottle. This also works with smashed garlic cloves. You can use the infused olive oil as a dipping oil for bread or vegetables, or drizzle it over pizzas, salads, or soups for that finishing touch.

Roast your vegetables. Roasting vegetables is the easiest way to cook them. The oven's heat caramelizes the natural sugars in the vegetables and brings out their sweet, nutty flavors. Just toss your favorite veggies with a little olive oil, salt, and pepper and roast them in a 400°F oven until crispy and fork-tender.

Season well! One of the biggest mistakes made in the kitchen is only seasoning your meal at the end of cooking. To get the most flavor impact, taste your dish at various steps in the process (just don't burn your tongue!) and add salt, pepper, and other spices as you go.

CHAPTER 2
SNACKS AND SMALL PLATES

HUMMUS

30 MINUTES OR LESS ✦ GLUTEN FREE ✦ NUT FREE ✦ VEGAN

PREP TIME: 20 MINUTES • SERVES 4

While I was growing up, my mom would hand me a beautiful bowl and a few lira and send me out the door to get hummus from our local hummus shop. The shop owner would mash the chickpeas and prepare the hummus, tasting it at every step. When he liked the flavor, he would spoon the hummus into my bowl, and garnish it with a few chickpeas, a sprinkle of black pepper, and a dash of paprika before handing it to me and sending me back home to my mother.

1 (15-ounce) can chickpeas, drained and rinsed

½ cup plus 3 tablespoons cold water, divided

4 garlic cloves, peeled

½ teaspoon ground cumin

¼ cup tahini

½ cup freshly squeezed lemon juice

Salt

1. In a food processor, combine the chickpeas, ½ cup of cold water, and garlic. Process for about 5 minutes or until well combined.
2. Add the cumin, tahini, and lemon juice and season with salt. Process into a smooth, spreadable paste, about 2 minutes more. If your hummus is a little thick, add more cold water, 1 tablespoon at a time, and process until it reaches the desired consistency.
3. Taste the hummus and season with more salt, as needed.

PER SERVING: CALORIES: 203; TOTAL FAT: 10G; SATURATED FAT: 2G; CARBOHYDRATES: 22G; FIBER: 6G; PROTEIN: 9G; SODIUM: 67MG

VARIATION TIP: To make sweet potato hummus, you will need 2 sweet potatoes, 1 tablespoon grated peeled fresh ginger, 2 peeled garlic cloves, ¼ cup freshly squeezed lemon juice, grated zest of 1 lemon, ¼ cup tahini, ¼ teaspoon ground cumin, and ⅛ teaspoon salt. Peel and wrap the potatoes, ginger, and garlic in aluminum foil. Place the packet on a baking sheet and bake in a 395°F oven for 1 hour. Remove from the oven, mash or process together, and stir in the lemon juice, lemon zest, tahini, cumin, and salt.

EGGPLANT CAVIAR

FREEZER FRIENDLY ✦ GLUTEN FREE ✦ NUT FREE ✦ VEGAN

PREP TIME: 10 MINUTES • COOK TIME: 10 MINUTES • CHILL TIME: 1 HOUR • SERVES 4

This dish is similar to baba ghanuj but is even easier to make. Sometimes called "poor's man caviar," the eggplant pulp gives this dip a similar appearance to the expensive appetizer, but it has the deliciously smoky taste of roasted eggplant instead of the briny tang of fish eggs. Sometimes this spread is made with plain yogurt in place of the tahini for a different flavor profile and color. Serve it with toasted pita bread and impress your guests.

2 (1-pound) eggplants

2 garlic cloves, mashed

½ cup finely chopped fresh parsley

½ cup finely diced red bell pepper

¼ cup freshly squeezed lemon juice, plus more as needed

2 tablespoons tahini

⅛ teaspoon salt, plus more as needed

PREP TIP: You can grill the eggplants instead. Pierce the eggplants in a few places with a fork. Grill them over medium heat for 30 to 40 minutes, turning often until they are evenly charred and the insides are soft. Let cool before peeling and following the instructions as written.

1. Preheat the broiler.
2. Pierce the eggplants with a fork in several places to prevent them from bursting in the oven, and place them on a rimmed baking sheet. Broil for about 3 minutes until the skin is charred on one side. Flip the eggplants and broil the other side for about 3 minutes more until charred. Remove and let cool.
3. Carefully remove the skin from the eggplants and scoop the pulp into a bowl. Using a fork or wooden pestle, mash the pulp into a smooth purée.
4. Add the garlic, parsley, red bell pepper, lemon juice, tahini, and salt. Stir until well combined. Taste and season with more salt, as needed.
5. Refrigerate for at least 1 hour before serving. Leftover "caviar" can be kept refrigerated in an airtight container for up to 5 days, or frozen for up to 1 month. Thaw in the refrigerator overnight before using.

PER SERVING: CALORIES: 115; TOTAL FAT: 5G; SATURATED FAT: 1G; CARBOHYDRATES: 17G; FIBER: 9G; PROTEIN: 4G; SODIUM: 95MG

WALNUT AND RED PEPPER SPREAD

30 MINUTES OR LESS ✦ FREEZER FRIENDLY ✦ VEGAN

PREP TIME: 20 MINUTES • SERVES 6

Also known as *muhammara*, this sweet and savory spread originated in Aleppo, Syria. It can be used as a topping for grilled vegetables or mixed with hummus to create an altogether different delight. A key ingredient is harissa, a popular Middle Eastern red pepper paste. It is widely available in Middle Eastern stores and online, or you can make your own from the recipe in this book.

3 slices whole-wheat bread

1 red bell pepper, seeded and coarsely chopped

½ onion, chopped

1 cup walnuts

3 tablespoons Harissa (page 143, or see tip), or store-bought

2 tablespoons pomegranate molasses, or cranberry juice

½ teaspoon ground coriander

½ teaspoon ground cumin

¼ cup olive oil

1. In a food processor, combine the bread, red bell pepper, onion, and walnuts.
2. Process for a few seconds until combined but coarse. Do not overprocess. You want to retain some texture of the walnuts in this spread.
3. Add the harissa, molasses, coriander, cumin, and olive oil. Process for a few seconds until the mixture resembles an almost smooth paste.
4. Refrigerate any leftovers in an airtight container for up to 1 week, or freeze for 2 to 3 months.

PER SERVING: CALORIES: 300; TOTAL FAT: 24G; SATURATED FAT: 3G; CARBOHYDRATES: 19G; FIBER: 3G; PROTEIN: 6G; SODIUM: 160MG

SUBSTITUTION TIP: If you can't find harissa at your local grocery store or don't want to make your own, substitute ¼ teaspoon cayenne pepper and 2 tablespoons freshly squeezed lemon juice.

GREEN OLIVE TAPENADE

30 MINUTES OR LESS ✦ GLUTEN FREE ✦ VEGAN

PREP TIME: 20 MINUTES • SERVES 6

Tapenade was originally made with only capers and olives, but in this recipe, I substitute walnuts and onion for the capers to provide a different flavor and texture experience. The olives are key and influence the final flavor of the tapenade. Serve this spread with a thinly sliced French baguette or mix it with cream cheese to create a fantastic topping for your bagel.

2 cups pitted green olives

1 cup coarsely chopped walnuts

1 onion, chopped

½ cup chopped fresh parsley

¼ cup freshly squeezed lemon juice

¼ cup olive oil

1 teaspoon dried oregano

1. In a food processor, combine the olives, walnuts, onion, and parsley. Pulse about 5 times until the mixture is coarsely chopped.
2. Add the lemon juice, olive oil, and oregano. Process for a few seconds more. The spread should be finely chopped but not puréed.

PER SERVING: CALORIES: 259; TOTAL FAT: 26G; SATURATED FAT: 3G; CARBOHYDRATES: 8G; FIBER: 3G; PROTEIN: 4G; SODIUM: 409MG

VARIATION TIP: I like to use pimento-stuffed olives, but you can make black olive tapenade using pitted Kalamata olives, if you prefer.

SKORDALIA

30 MINUTES OR LESS ✦ FREEZER FRIENDLY ✦ NUT FREE ✦ VEGAN

PREP TIME: 30 MINUTES • SERVES 6

If you love garlic, this recipe is for you! Skordalia is a thick spread from Greece tradition-ally made by combining a delectably large amount of garlic with a base. The base can be puréed potatoes, liquid-soaked bread, walnuts, or a combination of things, as I chose to do in this recipe. Skordalia pairs well with roasted vegetables and crunchy crackers.

1 cup water

5 large slices Italian bread, crusts removed

8 garlic cloves, peeled

⅛ teaspoon salt, plus more as needed

4 potatoes, peeled and boiled

½ cup apple cider vinegar, plus more as needed

½ cup olive oil

1. Pour the water onto a rimmed baking sheet and put the bread slices into the water. Soak the bread for 5 minutes. Remove the bread and squeeze out the excess water. Set aside.
2. In a medium bowl, using a fork or wooden pestle, mash the garlic and salt into a smooth paste. Add the boiled potatoes and soaked bread and gently mash and mix to combine.
3. Add the vinegar and olive oil and continue to mix until you have no lumps. Slowly mix in more vinegar if the skordalia is too thick to spread. Taste and season with more salt, as needed.
4. Cover and refrigerate until serving. Spoon any leftovers into an airtight container and freeze for up to 1 month.

PER SERVING: CALORIES: 320; TOTAL FAT: 18G; SATURATED FAT: 3G; CARBOHYDRATES: 36G; FIBER: 4G; PROTEIN: 5G; SODIUM: 207MG

VARIATION TIP: The skordalia can be made using only pota-toes if you are allergic to gluten.

MINT LABNEH

GLUTEN FREE ✦ NUT FREE

PREP TIME: 10 MINUTES • DRAIN TIME: 2 HOURS • SERVES 6

Labneh is the cream cheese of the Mediterranean. You can mix this with puréed fresh mint, as I do here, for a wonderful spread, or with za'atar and olive oil for a different flavor profile. Serve this spread with pita bread or fresh veggies for dipping, or use it to top crostini. I recommend cheesecloth to make this recipe, but if you don't have that, any fine-mesh fabric will do. My mom used an old pillowcase that she would wash and reuse anytime she wanted to make this!

32 ounces Plain Yogurt (page 150), or store-bought

½ teaspoon salt

¼ cup olive oil

¼ cup finely chopped fresh mint

1. In a large bowl, stir together the yogurt and salt.
2. Line a colander with several layers of cheesecloth. Spoon the yogurt mixture into the lined colander. Place the colander over a sink or a bowl and let the mixture sit for 2 hours or until most of the water is drained.
3. Spoon the labneh into a small bowl and stir in the olive oil and mint until well combined. The labneh can be refrigerated in an airtight container for 1 to 2 weeks.

PER SERVING: CALORIES: 173; TOTAL FAT: 14G; SATURATED FAT: 5G; CARBOHYDRATES: 8G; FIBER: 0G; PROTEIN: 5G; SODIUM: 233MG

SWEET AND SOUR BEET DIP

GLUTEN FREE ✦ NUT FREE ✦ VEGAN

PREP TIME: 10 MINUTES • COOK TIME: 50 MINUTES • SERVES 6

Because of the colorful use of beets in this dip, my customers call it the "beautiful hummus." Not only is it beautiful, it is healthy, too! Beets are an excellent source of antioxidants and nitrates. Nitrates help lower blood pressure and heart rate and antioxidants help protect our body's cells from damage. On top of that, it tastes great. The beets give the dip a sweet, earthy flavor that combines with the nuttiness of the tahini and the spicy zing from the cayenne pepper. This dip is the perfect accompaniment to freshly baked Pita Bread (page 152).

1 pound beets, trimmed

½ cup tahini

½ cup freshly squeezed lemon juice

4 garlic cloves, mashed

Grated zest of 1 lemon

1 teaspoon ground cumin

¼ teaspoon cayenne pepper

Salt

Freshly ground black pepper

1. In a large saucepan, combine the beets with enough water to cover. Place the pan over high heat and boil the beets for about 50 minutes or until tender, adding more water as needed to keep them submerged.
2. Drain the beets, let them cool, and peel them. The skins should slide off easily.
3. Transfer the beets to a food processor and purée for about 5 minutes until smooth. Transfer the puréed beets to a medium bowl.
4. Stir in the tahini, lemon juice, garlic, lemon zest, cumin, and cayenne until well mixed. Taste and season with salt and black pepper, as needed.

PER SERVING: CALORIES: 162; TOTAL FAT: 11G; SATURATED FAT: 2G; CARBOHYDRATES: 13G; FIBER: 4G; PROTEIN: 5G; SODIUM: 113MG

MARINATED OLIVES

GLUTEN FREE ✦ NUT FREE ✦ VEGAN

PREP TIME: 10 MINUTES • MARINATE TIME: 3 HOURS • SERVES 4

Marinated olives are a staple in every kitchen around the Mediterranean. In this recipe I use green olives, but you can use black olives, Kalamata olives, small olives, large olives—the result of any combination will be delicious. If you use unpitted olives, beware when you take a bite! Don't discard the oil that's left over after you finish the olives. Serve it with some crusty bread for dipping.

¼ cup olive oil

¼ cup red wine vinegar

Grated zest of 1 lemon

1 teaspoon chopped
   fresh rosemary

2 cups jarred olives, drained

1. In a medium bowl, whisk the olive oil, vinegar, lemon zest, and rosemary until blended.
2. Add the olives and gently stir to coat. Toss well and let marinate for at least 3 hours before serving.

PER SERVING: CALORIES: 209; TOTAL FAT: 21G; SATURATED FAT: 3G; CARBOHYDRATES: 7G; FIBER: 3G; PROTEIN: 1G; SODIUM: 978MG

VARIATION TIP: Add fresh lemon slices or a pinch of spice, like fennel seed or coriander seed.

MARINATED ZUCCHINI

GLUTEN FREE ✦ NUT FREE ✦ VEGAN

PREP TIME: 15 MINUTES • COOK TIME: 5 MINUTES
MARINATE TIME: 30 MINUTES • SERVES 6

You can use this zesty marinade on almost any vegetable—from eggplant to bell peppers to mushrooms. Delectable both warm and straight from the refrigerator, this zucchini is perfect for a healthy snack. If you have one available, use an outdoor grill turned to medium-high heat to cook the zucchini to add a smokier flavor.

¼ cup balsamic vinegar

2 tablespoons stone-ground mustard

1 garlic clove, minced

2 teaspoons chopped fresh thyme

¼ cup olive oil

⅛ teaspoon salt

⅛ teaspoon freshly ground black pepper

3 large zucchini, cut diagonally into ½-inch-thick slices

1. In a small bowl, whisk the vinegar, mustard, garlic, and thyme to combine. Gradually whisk in the olive oil until blended. Season with the salt and pepper and whisk again to combine.
2. Place the zucchini in a large bowl and drizzle ¼ cup of marinade over them. Toss well to coat.
3. Heat a grill pan or sauté pan over medium heat.
4. Place the zucchini slices in the pan. Cook for about 5 minutes, turning occasionally, until the zucchini is tender and lightly charred.
5. Transfer the cooked zucchini back to the bowl and drizzle it with the remaining marinade. Toss to coat. Cover the bowl and refrigerate the zucchini to marinate for 30 minutes or until chilled.
6. Arrange the marinated slices on a serving platter and drizzle with the marinade from the bowl to serve.

PER SERVING: CALORIES: 105; TOTAL FAT: 9G; SATURATED FAT: 1G; CARBOHYDRATES: 6G; FIBER: 2G; PROTEIN: 2G; SODIUM: 90MG

PICKLED TURNIPS

GLUTEN FREE ✦ NUT FREE ✦ VEGAN

PREP TIME: 15 MINUTES • PICKLING TIME: 1 WEEK • SERVES 12

Legend has it that Queen Cleopatra of Egypt credited the pickles in her diet with contributing to her storied beauty. You can put this theory to the test with these easy pickled turnips that will be hard not to eat right out of the jar! Although beets aren't a necessary ingredient, they add a unique and striking color.

4 cups water

¼ cup salt

1 cup white distilled vinegar

1 small beet, peeled
and quartered

1 garlic clove, peeled

2 pounds turnips, peeled,
halved, and cut into
¼-inch half-moons

1. In a medium bowl, whisk the water and salt until the salt dissolves. Whisk in the vinegar.
2. Place the beet and garlic in a clean 2-quart glass jar with a tight-sealing lid. Layer the turnips on top.
3. Pour the vinegar mixture over the turnips to cover them. Seal the lid tightly and let the jar sit at room temperature for 1 week.

PER SERVING: CALORIES: 26; TOTAL FAT: 0G; SATURATED FAT: 0G; CARBOHYDRATES: 6G; FIBER: 1G; PROTEIN: 1G; SODIUM: 212MG

PREP TIP: Beets stain hands and clothes, so wear gloves and an apron when you peel and cut them.

STORAGE TIP: The pickles are ready to eat after 1 week, but they can be stored in the pantry for up to 1 month and kept refrigerated for up to 1 year.

A TALE OF TAPAS

It is often disputed exactly how the concept of tapas, or mezza, began. Some say it originated in the small bars of Seville, where bartenders would place a few olives and slices of cheese on small plates on top of the wineglasses to keep the flies out. Others believe restaurants began serving tapas to prevent customers from getting too tipsy on empty stomachs before their main dishes arrived.

Whatever the origin, in the Mediterranean, tapas are often more important than the main course. When eating out, it's typical to walk into the restaurant, order a drink, and choose a number of tapas before even sitting down. These could include things like Marinated Olives (page 17), Tomato and Basil Bruschetta (page 28), Patatas Bravas (page 23), and a wide assortment of dips accompanied by fresh pita bread.

Similar to appetizers in America but smaller in portion size, the mezza dishes are placed in the middle of the table for everyone to enjoy. In spring and summer months, most tapas are to be enjoyed outside and are often served cold to provide a small sense of relief against the Mediterranean heat. Once served, people take their time savoring these small dishes, drinking, and enjoying the conversation. Diners have so much fun with the medley of mezza, they often continue to order them until they become a full meal!

BRAISED SWEET PEPPERS

GLUTEN FREE ✦ NUT FREE ✦ VEGAN

PREP TIME: 10 MINUTES • COOK TIME: 40 MINUTES • SERVES 4

Bell peppers are very low in calories yet are an excellent source of vitamins and antioxidants. To best preserve the healthy benefits of peppers, I suggest braising them. When braising, the vegetables are cooked "low and slow" in a flavorful liquid such as broth or wine. You will also find that braising vegetables intensifies their flavor. After trying these peppers, braise carrots, fennel, and even cabbage. You are in for a delicious treat!

¼ cup olive oil

1 red onion, thinly sliced

3 red bell peppers, seeded and cut into 1-inch strips

3 green bell peppers, seeded and cut into 1-inch strips

2 garlic cloves, chopped

¼ teaspoon cayenne pepper

⅛ teaspoon salt

⅛ teaspoon freshly ground black pepper

¼ cup vegetable broth

1 tablespoon chopped fresh thyme

1. In a large saucepan over medium heat, heat the olive oil.
2. Add the red onion and cook for 5 minutes.
3. Add the red and green bell peppers, garlic, cayenne, salt, and black pepper.
4. Pour in the vegetable broth and bring the mixture to a boil. Cover the pan and reduce the heat to low. Cook for 35 minutes, stirring occasionally, until the vegetables are soft but still firm.
5. Sprinkle the peppers with the thyme and serve.

PER SERVING: CALORIES: 184; TOTAL FAT: 15G; SATURATED FAT: 2G; CARBOHYDRATES: 15G; FIBER: 4G; PROTEIN: 3G; SODIUM: 128MG

SUBSTITUTION TIP: Use 1 teaspoon dried thyme instead of fresh and add it when you add the cayenne.

CARAMELIZED PEARL ONIONS

30 MINUTES OR LESS ✦ GLUTEN FREE ✦ NUT FREE ✦ VEGAN

PREP TIME: 5 MINUTES • COOK TIME: 15 MINUTES • SERVES 4

This classic French appetizer is a snap to make! Packed with antioxidants, and a tasty addition to any meal, they'll become a frequent request. Although fantastic to serve as a stand-alone dish, these onions taste even better when accompanied by aged cheeses such as Gruyère, Manchego, or Parmesan. I love to use them as a topping for pizza.

¼ cup olive oil

1 pound frozen pearl onions, thawed

3 tablespoons sugar

½ cup balsamic vinegar

1 tablespoon chopped fresh rosemary

⅛ teaspoon salt

⅛ teaspoon red pepper flakes

1. In a medium sauté pan or skillet over medium heat, heat the olive oil.
2. Add the onions and cook for about 5 minutes until they begin to brown.
3. Add the sugar and cook for about 5 minutes more until the sugar is caramelized, gently stirring so the onions do not stick to the pan.
4. Add the vinegar and rosemary. Cook for about 2 minutes, stirring occasionally, until a syrup forms.
5. Stir in the salt and red pepper flakes. Remove from the heat and let cool before serving.

PER SERVING: CALORIES: 203; TOTAL FAT: 14G; SATURATED FAT: 2G; CARBOHYDRATES: 18G; FIBER: 1G; PROTEIN: 13G; SODIUM: 89MG

PREP TIP: Ever wonder how to judge when the oil in the pan is ready for your ingredients? Pour the oil into the pan, place a small slice of onion in the cold oil, turn on the heat, and when the onion starts to sizzle, the oil is ready for cooking!

PATATAS BRAVAS

30 MINUTES OR LESS ✦ NUT FREE ✦ VEGAN

PREP TIME: 10 MINUTES • COOK TIME: 20 MINUTES • SERVES 4

These simple and spicy potatoes are one of Spain's most popular tapas, and you'll find them on the menu in every restaurant. Although the dish has only two main components—potatoes and the sauce—it's anything but boring. The sauce is the star: smoky, spicy, and sweet. It's a flavor explosion. It's my belief that the potatoes are really just a vehicle to get the sauce into your mouth!

2 cups olive oil, divided

1 tablespoon cayenne pepper, plus more as needed

2 tablespoons sweet paprika, plus more as needed

1 tablespoon all-purpose flour

1 cup vegetable broth

⅛ teaspoon salt, plus more as needed

4 russet or Yukon Gold potatoes, peeled, cut into 1-inch cubes, and patted dry

1. In a small saucepan over medium heat, heat ¼ cup of olive oil for about 2 minutes until warm. Remove from the heat and whisk in the cayenne, paprika, and flour until you have a paste.
2. Add the vegetable broth and salt. Return the saucepan to medium-low heat and cook the mixture for about 5 minutes, stirring constantly, until it thickens into a sauce. Taste and adjust the seasoning. Remove from the heat and set the sauce aside.
3. In a large skillet over medium heat, heat the remaining 1¾ cups of olive oil.
4. Gently add the potatoes and fry for about 10 minutes, stirring occasionally, until crispy and golden. Using a slotted spoon, transfer the potatoes to paper towels to drain. Transfer the potatoes to a serving platter and drizzle with the sauce.

PER SERVING: CALORIES: 394; TOTAL FAT: 27G; SATURATED FAT: 4G; CARBOHYDRATES: 38G; FIBER: 7G; PROTEIN: 6G; SODIUM: 279MG

PREP TIP: You can also toss the potatoes in the olive oil, place them on a baking sheet, and bake in a 400°F oven for 30 minutes or until golden brown and fork-tender.

STUFFED GRAPE LEAVES

FREEZER FRIENDLY ✦ GLUTEN FREE ✦ NUT FREE ✦ VEGAN

PREP TIME: 40 MINUTES • COOK TIME: 1 HOUR, 5 MINUTES • MAKES 60 GRAPE LEAVES

This recipe uses rice and herbs to keep things vegetarian and vegan friendly, but grape leaves can be stuffed with ground lamb and rice, which is a popular main dish in Eastern Mediterranean countries. I have a secret weapon for making this: The potato slices on the bottom of the pot prevent the stuffed grape leaves from sticking, ensuring your finished product stays intact.

½ cup plus 1 tablespoon olive oil, divided

1 onion, finely chopped

1½ cups short-grain rice

6 cups cold water, divided

1 cup finely chopped fresh parsley

10 garlic cloves, peeled

2 tomatoes, finely chopped

1 teaspoon ground allspice

Salt

Freshly ground black pepper

1 (16-ounce) can grape leaves, drained, rinsed, stems cut off

4 potatoes, peeled and cut into ½-inch-thick rounds

½ cup freshly squeezed lemon juice

1. In a skillet over medium-low heat, heat ¼ cup of olive oil.
2. Add the onion and sauté for 5 minutes.
3. Stir in the rice and cook for 1 minute.
4. Stir in 2 cups of cold water and cook for 5 minutes, or until the water evaporates. Remove from the heat and stir in the parsley, 3 cloves of the garlic (minced), tomatoes, and allspice and season with salt and pepper. Transfer the rice mixture to a bowl and set aside.
5. Place the grape leaves, shiny-side down, on a work surface. Spoon 1 tablespoon of the stuffing into the center of each leaf.
6. Fold the stem side horizontally over the stuffing, then fold the 2 vertical sides over the first fold; roll tightly until it reaches the leaf point, forming a cylinder 2 inches long by 1 inch thick.
7. Cover the bottom of a heavy round pot with the potato slices and drizzle with 1 tablespoon of olive oil.
8. Layer the stuffed grape leaves, tightly side by side, on top of the potato slices. Each layer will have about 30 stuffed leaves. Arrange the remaining 7 garlic cloves between them. Drizzle with the remaining ¼ cup of olive oil.
9. Place a round flat glass plate on top of the rolls and press down lightly. The plate should be slightly smaller than the pot, leaving about ¼ inch between the plate and the pot's edge.

10. Add the remaining 4 cups of cold water. The water should cover the plate and the grape leaves, and decrease as the grape leaves cook.
11. Place the pot over medium heat and cook for 15 minutes. Turn the heat to low and cook for 40 minutes more.
12. Remove the pot from the heat, carefully remove the plate, and drizzle the grape leaves with the lemon juice. Cover and let cool before serving.

PER SERVING: (5 LEAVES) CALORIES: 270; TOTAL FAT: 12G; SATURATED FAT: 2G; CARBOHYDRATES: 39G; FIBER: 3G; PROTEIN: 5G; SODIUM: 888MG

MAKE AHEAD: Arrange the uncooked stuffed grape leaves in a freezer-safe container, seal well, and freeze for up to 2 months. When ready to use, remove from the freezer, arrange in a pot over the potato slices, and follow the same steps to cook. No need to thaw!

INGREDIENT TIP: If using fresh grape leaves, blanch them in very hot water for about 10 seconds, just to soften.

FILO-WRAPPED BRIE WITH ORANGE MARMALADE

FREEZER FRIENDLY ✦ NUT FREE

PREP TIME: 30 MINUTES • COOK TIME: 30 MINUTES • SERVES 12

This unique and elegant recipe is sure to make any occasion feel fancy. Creamy Brie is smothered in sweet orange marmalade, wrapped in filo dough, and baked to golden perfection. It's sure to be a showstopper. You can prepare the ingredients a day before baking, or you can make it, wrap it well with aluminum foil, and freeze for up to 1 month. If you decide to make it ahead, thaw in the refrigerator overnight before baking and serving.

4 tablespoons butter, melted

6 (18-by-14-inch) sheets frozen filo dough, thawed; follow the instruction on the package to prevent drying

1 (14-ounce) wheel Brie cheese, unwrapped, rind left on

½ cup orange marmalade

Crackers, for serving

1. Preheat the oven to 400°F.
2. Brush a baking sheet with melted butter. Place 1 sheet of filo dough on the baking sheet; brush it lightly with melted butter. Place another filo sheet on top; brush it lightly with melted butter. Repeat the same process until you finish with all 6 pieces of dough.
3. Place the cheese wheel in the center of the filo dough stack. Spoon and spread the orange marmalade over the cheese.
4. Gently fold the filo dough over the cheese and marmalade until the cheese is completely covered. Press gently to seal. Brush the filo bundle with the remaining melted butter.
5. Bake for 20 minutes or until golden brown. Let cool for 10 minutes and serve with crackers.

PER SERVING: CALORIES: 205; TOTAL FAT: 14G; SATURATED FAT: 8G; CARBOHYDRATES: 14G; FIBER: 0G; PROTEIN: 8G; SODIUM: 288MG

SUBSTITUTION TIP: Use frozen puff pastry instead of filo dough.

VARIATION TIP: Instead of orange, use any flavor of marmalade or jam for a different spin on this delicious recipe.

SPINACH AND WALNUT FATAYERS

FREEZER FRIENDLY ✦ VEGAN

PREP TIME: 30 MINUTES • COOK TIME: 15 MINUTES • MAKES 12 FATAYERS

Fatayers, pronounced like "fat tires," are delicious pockets of stuffed dough baked until they are golden brown. They are the Middle Eastern version of empanadas and calzones. Their size makes them perfect to enjoy for a snack—or eat a few as a main course.

2 (10-ounce) packages fresh spinach, chopped

¼ teaspoon salt, plus more for sprinkling

1 small onion, finely chopped

¼ cup coarsely chopped walnuts

¼ cup olive oil

½ teaspoon ground sumac (see tip)

½ yield Pizza Dough (page 153), or 1 pound store-bought, thawed, at room temperature

All-purpose flour, for dusting

1. Preheat the oven to 375°F.
2. Place the spinach in a medium bowl and sprinkle it with salt. Gently massage the spinach and let sit for 5 minutes. Squeeze out the excess moisture and return the spinach to the bowl.
3. Add the onion, walnuts, olive oil, sumac, and salt. Stir to combine and set aside.
4. Cut the dough into 12 balls. Lightly flour a work surface and roll out the dough balls on it into ⅛-inch-thick circles.
5. Place 1 heaping tablespoon of the spinach stuffing in the center of each circle. Fold up the sides to the center, squeezing them to seal and form a triangle. Arrange the fatayers on a baking sheet.
6. Bake for 15 minutes or until the fatayers are golden brown.

PER SERVING: (1 FATAYER) CALORIES: 149; TOTAL FAT: 8G; SATURATED FAT: 1G; CARBOHYDRATES: 18G; FIBER: 3G; PROTEIN: 4G; SODIUM: 247MG

LEFTOVERS TIP: You can bake and freeze these fatayers for up to 1 month. Place them in a freezer-safe plastic bag, take out as many as you need, and let them thaw overnight in the refrigerator. Bake in a 250°F oven for 2 to 3 minutes to warm.

SUBSTITUTION TIP: If you don't have sumac, use an equal amount of lemon zest mixed with a pinch of salt.

TOMATO AND BASIL BRUSCHETTA

30 MINUTES OR LESS ✦ NUT FREE ✦ VEGAN

PREP TIME: 15 MINUTES • COOK TIME: 5 MINUTES • SERVES 4

Bruschetta is extremely versatile—and extremely delicious! This version is a simple way to use all the extra tomatoes from your garden during summer. You can make caprese bruschetta by adding fresh mozzarella to this recipe or, for different Mediterranean flavors, combine labneh and mint or diced strawberries and feta. Here I've taken the standard approach of topping the bread before serving, but my favorite way to serve bruschetta is to spoon the tomato mixture into a bowl and place the garlic bread around it.

2 tablespoons olive oil

2 garlic cloves, mashed

½ baguette, cut into 12 slices

3 small ripe tomatoes, seeded and chopped

1 cup chopped fresh basil

Salt

Pepper

1. Preheat the broiler.
2. In a small bowl, stir together the olive oil and garlic. Brush the bread slices with this mixture and place them on a baking sheet. Set aside.
3. In another small bowl, stir together the tomatoes and basil and season with salt and pepper. Taste, and adjust seasoning, if needed.
4. Place the bread under the broiler for 1 minute until crisp and lightly toasted. Remove from the oven, spoon 1 tablespoon of the tomato mixture on top of each piece slice, and serve.

PER SERVING: CALORIES: 206; TOTAL FAT: 8G; SATURATED FAT: 1G; CARBOHYDRATES: 28G; FIBER: 2G; PROTEIN: 6G; SODIUM: 313MG

GOAT CHEESE AND HONEY CROSTINI

30 MINUTES OR LESS ✦ NUT FREE

PREP TIME: 10 MINUTES • COOK TIME: 10 MINUTES • SERVES 4

Crostini, which means "little toast" in Italian, are similar to bruschetta and make excellent finger foods. This is a sweeter version, but you can also make savory crostini by topping your toasts with sun-dried tomatoes, black olive paste, or Green Olive Tapenade (page 13). The best bread to use is one on the denser side, but use whatever you have on hand.

½ baguette, cut into 12 thin slices

4 tablespoons olive oil, divided

¼ teaspoon salt

4 ounces goat cheese, at room temperature

½ teaspoon dried thyme

4 tablespoons honey

1. Preheat the oven to 375°F.
2. Place the bread slices on a baking sheet. Brush with 2 tablespoons of olive oil. Sprinkle with the salt and bake for 10 minutes or until lightly toasted. Remove and set aside.
3. In a medium bowl, stir together the goat cheese, the remaining 2 tablespoons of olive oil, and the thyme.
4. Arrange the toast on a platter and spread with the goat cheese. Drizzle with the honey and serve.

PER SERVING: CALORIES: 358; TOTAL FAT: 20G; SATURATED FAT: 6G; CARBOHYDRATES: 36G; FIBER: 1G; PROTEIN: 9G; SODIUM: 218MG

CHAPTER 3
SOUPS, SALADS, AND SANDWICHES

RIBOLLITA

NUT FREE

PREP TIME: 15 MINUTES • COOK TIME: 1 HOUR • SERVES 8

Bread is never wasted in the Mediterranean kitchen! In this recipe, bread that is going stale can be put to good use to thicken the soup. This delicious dish is a savory way to warm up in winter. Full of protein, carbs, fiber, and dairy, ribollita is a meal on its own.

1 potato, peeled and cut into 1-inch cubes

½ cup olive oil, divided

1 teaspoon red pepper flakes

1 onion, chopped

4 celery stalks, chopped

1 carrot, diced

4 garlic cloves, mashed

1 (28-ounce) can crushed tomatoes

¼ cup tomato paste

6 cups water

1 tablespoon dried basil

Salt

2 cups shredded cabbage

2 cups coarsely chopped Swiss chard

1 zucchini, cut into 1-inch cubes

1 (16-ounce) can kidney beans, drained and rinsed

2 cups (1-inch) bread cubes

½ cup freshly grated Parmesan cheese (optional)

1. In a medium bowl, combine the potato cubes with enough cold water to cover and set aside.
2. In a small bowl, whisk ¼ cup of olive oil and the red pepper flakes. Set aside.
3. In a large soup pot over low heat, heat the remaining ¼ cup of olive oil.
4. Add the onion, celery, and carrot. Stir to coat with the oil and cook for 5 minutes or until the vegetables begin to soften.
5. Stir in the garlic, tomatoes, tomato paste, water, and basil. Bring to a boil, taste, and season with salt, as needed.
6. Drain the potato cubes and add them to the pot. Cook for 5 minutes.
7. Add the cabbage, chard, and zucchini. Return the soup to a boil before reducing the heat to low and simmering for 20 minutes.
8. Stir in the kidney beans and cook for 5 minutes more. Turn off the heat. Add the bread cubes and stir to combine. Let the soup rest for 15 minutes. Turn the heat to medium and cook for about 5 minutes until warmed through.
9. Spoon into bowls, drizzle with the reserved red pepper flakes and olive oil, and top with the Parmesan cheese (if using).

PER SERVING: CALORIES: 244; TOTAL FAT: 13G; SATURATED FAT: 2G; CARBOHYDRATES: 27G; FIBER: 8G; PROTEIN: 7G; SODIUM: 298MG

LENTIL SOUP

NUT FREE ✦ VEGAN

PREP TIME: 15 MINUTES • COOK TIME: 35 MINUTES • SERVES 6

The lentil is a very inexpensive, highly nutritious legume that has the added benefit of taking only a short time to cook. Nearly every country and region surrounding the Mediterranean has its own lentil soup recipe, and they are all delicious. This one reminds me of the one I ate while growing up, and I hope it warms you as much as the memories that come with it warm me.

¼ cup olive oil

1 onion, finely chopped

2 celery stalks, chopped

2 carrots, diced

4 garlic cloves, mashed

¼ cup tomato paste

½ teaspoon paprika

½ teaspoon ground cumin

10 cups water

2 cups dried brown lentils, rinsed and picked over for debris

⅛ teaspoon salt

½ cup short-grain rice

1 tablespoon Harissa (page 143), or store-bought

¼ cup chopped fresh cilantro

¼ cup freshly squeezed lemon juice

Toasted pita chips, for serving

1. In a large soup pot over medium-high heat, heat the olive oil.
2. Add the onion, celery, and carrots. Cook for 5 minutes.
3. Add the garlic, tomato paste, paprika, and cumin. Mix well and stir in the water. Bring to a boil.
4. Add the lentils and salt. Return the mixture to a boil, lower the heat to medium, and simmer for 15 minutes.
5. Add the rice and harissa. Return the soup to a boil and simmer for 10 minutes.
6. Stir in the cilantro and lemon juice. Reduce the heat to low and cook for 5 minutes. Serve with toasted pita chips.

PER SERVING: CALORIES: 393; TOTAL FAT: 11G; SATURATED FAT: 2G; CARBOHYDRATES: 59G; FIBER: 9G; PROTEIN: 18G; SODIUM: 130MG

VARIATION TIP: To make a lentil soup traditionally found in Turkey, Syria, and Lebanon, use orange lentils and skip the harissa and cilantro.

POTATO LEEK SOUP

GLUTEN FREE ✦ NUT FREE

PREP TIME: 20 MINUTES • COOK TIME: 45 MINUTES • SERVES 8

The cream and butter make this French staple a decadently rich meal, but replacing the butter with olive oil and forgoing the cream easily yields a lighter, dairy-free option.

5 russet potatoes, peeled and cut into 1-inch cubes

8 cups vegetable broth

2 tablespoons butter

2 celery stalks, chopped

3 leeks, white parts only, washed and julienned

1 cup heavy cream

¼ cup chopped fresh tarragon

Salt

Freshly ground black pepper

1. In a large soup pot over medium-high heat, combine the potatoes and vegetable broth. Bring to a boil, reduce the heat to medium, and cook for 15 to 20 minutes until the potatoes are soft. Remove from the heat.
2. Using an immersion blender, blend until smooth. You can also purée the mixture in batches in a regular blender; just be careful, as the liquid will be extremely hot.
3. In a saucepan over medium heat, melt the butter. Add the celery and leeks and cook for about 5 minutes until tender.
4. Add the heavy cream and tarragon and cook for about 2 minutes until the cream is warmed through. Add the warm cream mixture to the potato mixture. Stir until well combined.
5. Place the soup back over medium heat. Taste, season with salt and pepper, as needed, and simmer the soup, stirring often, for 15 minutes or until warmed through.

PER SERVING: CALORIES: 372; TOTAL FAT: 16G; SATURATED FAT: 9G; CARBOHYDRATES: 49G; FIBER: 4G; PROTEIN: 11G; SODIUM: 214MG

SUBSTITUTION TIP: If you don't have fresh tarragon, use 1 teaspoon dried tarragon instead.

VEGETABLE AND CHICKPEA SOUP

GLUTEN FREE ✦ NUT FREE ✦ VEGAN

PREP TIME: 15 MINUTES • COOK TIME: 45 MINUTES • SERVES 6

This soup is the minestrone of the East. In Italy the soup contains cannellini beans and is flavored with fresh or dried basil; in this version I use chickpeas and mint for a unique spin. Serve this soup over rice for a more filling meal.

½ cup olive oil, divided

1 onion, finely chopped

½ cup tomato paste

10 cups water

1 (16-ounce) can crushed tomatoes

4 garlic cloves, mashed, divided

⅛ teaspoon salt

⅛ teaspoon freshly ground black pepper

2 potatoes, cut into ½-inch cubes

2 tomatoes, seeded and cut into 1-inch cubes

1 zucchini, cut into ½-inch cubes

4 cups fresh baby spinach

1 (15-ounce) can chickpeas, drained and rinsed

1 tablespoon dried mint

¼ cup freshly squeezed lemon juice

1. In a large soup pot over medium heat, heat ¼ cup of olive oil. Add the onion and cook for 5 minutes.
2. Add the tomato paste and 1 cup of water and stir until the paste dissolves. Add the remaining 9 cups of water, the crushed tomatoes, 2 garlic cloves, salt, and pepper. Bring to a boil.
3. Gently add the potatoes to the pot. Simmer for 5 minutes.
4. Add the tomatoes, zucchini, and spinach. Simmer for 15 minutes.
5. Add the chickpeas and cook for 5 minutes more.
6. In a small saucepan over medium-high heat, warm the remaining ¼ cup of olive oil.
7. Add the remaining 2 garlic cloves and sauté for 1 minute. Add the mint and cook for 1 minute more. Remove the saucepan from the heat, stir in the lemon juice, and pour the oil mixture into the soup pot. Stir until well mixed and simmer for 5 minutes before serving.

PER SERVING: CALORIES: 361; TOTAL FAT: 19G; SATURATED FAT: 3G; CARBOHYDRATES: 42G; FIBER: 11G; PROTEIN: 11G; SODIUM: 250MG

VARIATION TIP: For a more traditional minestrone soup, like the one found in Italy, replace the chickpeas with cannellini beans and replace the mint with basil. Top with grated Parmesan for added richness.

HARIRA SOUP

DAIRY FREE ✦ FREEZER FRIENDLY ✦ NUT FREE

PREP TIME: 30 MINUTES • COOK TIME: 40 MINUTES • SERVES 8

This soup gets its name from the Arabic word for "silk" because, once it has been thickened with the eggs, it's silky smooth.

¼ cup olive oil

1 large onion, chopped

3 celery stalks, chopped

2 large carrots, cut into thin rounds

1 tablespoon Harissa (page 143), or store-bought

1 tablespoon ground turmeric

1 teaspoon ground cumin

½ teaspoon ground cinnamon

1 cup chopped fresh cilantro, divided

1 cup chopped fresh parsley, divided

2 cups tomato sauce

10 cups water, divided

2 cups dried brown lentils, rinsed and picked over

1 (15-ounce) can chickpeas, drained and rinsed

⅛ teaspoon salt, plus more as needed

1 large egg

½ cup freshly squeezed lemon juice

2 tablespoons all-purpose flour

1 teaspoon grated peeled fresh ginger

1. In a large soup pot over medium heat, heat the olive oil.
2. Add the onion, celery, and carrots. Cook for 5 minutes.
3. Stir in the harissa, turmeric, cumin, cinnamon, ½ cup of cilantro, and ½ cup of parsley. Cook for 5 minutes.
4. Add the tomato sauce, 8 cups of water, and the lentils. Simmer, uncovered, for about 25 minutes until the lentils are cooked.
5. Stir in the chickpeas and salt.
6. In a medium bowl, whisk the egg, lemon juice, flour, ginger, and remaining 2 cups of water until well combined. Slowly stir the mixture into the soup.
7. Simmer the soup for 5 minutes more. Taste and season with more salt, as needed. Spoon into bowls and top with the remaining ½ cup each of cilantro and parsley.

PER SERVING: CALORIES: 358; TOTAL FAT: 11G; SATURATED FAT: 2G; CARBOHYDRATES: 51G; FIBER: 11G; PROTEIN: 19G; SODIUM: 308MG

LEFTOVERS TIP: Spoon leftovers into a freezer-safe container and freeze for up to 2 months. When ready to eat, thaw in the refrigerator before warming on the stovetop or in the microwave.

ROASTED RED BELL PEPPER SOUP

GLUTEN FREE ✦ NUT FREE ✦ VEGAN

PREP TIME: 45 MINUTES • COOK TIME: 35 MINUTES • SERVES 6

This delicious sweet and smoky soup is sure to become a winter staple. Although it might seem a bit time-consuming to roast the peppers yourself, I promise the finished product is worth the extra effort. This soup tastes great topped with salty feta or Parmesan cheese, if dairy is not a concern.

8 large red bell peppers, halved and seeded

¼ cup olive oil

1 onion, chopped

2 celery stalks, diced

4 garlic cloves, peeled

¼ cup tomato paste

4 cups vegetable broth

2 tablespoons chopped fresh oregano

¼ teaspoon cayenne pepper, plus more as needed

⅛ teaspoon salt, plus more as needed

1. Preheat the broiler.
2. Place the peppers, cut-side down, on a baking sheet and broil for about 10 minutes until charred.
3. Remove the peppers from the oven and carefully wrap them in a clean kitchen towel or place them in a paper bag. Let cool. Once cool, unwrap the peppers and peel off their skins.
4. Place the peppers in a food processor and purée into a semi-smooth liquid. Set aside.
5. In a medium soup pot over medium heat, heat the olive oil. Add the onion, celery, and garlic. Cook for 5 minutes or until the vegetables have softened.
6. Stir in the tomato paste, vegetable broth, oregano, and cayenne. Cook for 10 minutes.
7. Stir in the puréed peppers and salt. Taste and season with more cayenne or salt, as needed. Bring the soup to a boil. Reduce the heat to low and simmer for 10 minutes to let the flavors develop before serving.

PER SERVING: CALORIES: 155; TOTAL FAT: 10G; SATURATED FAT: 1G; CARBOHYDRATES: 18G; FIBER: 4G; PROTEIN: 3G; SODIUM: 71MG

PREP TIP: Use canned or jarred roasted red bell peppers instead of fresh peppers to reduce prep time.

FRENCH ONION SOUP

NUT FREE

PREP TIME: 15 MINUTES • COOK TIME: 1 HOUR • SERVES 6

Caramelized onions are fantastic on their own, but they're taken to the next level when partnered with an herby broth and salty Gruyère cheese. Because caramelizing onions is an experiment in patience, I always cook extra when I make this soup. Use them as a topping for fried eggs, mix them with cream cheese for your morning bagel, or just eat them as a snack.

3 tablespoons butter

5 large onions, thinly sliced

3 garlic cloves, mashed

Salt

6 cups vegetable broth

2 tablespoons apple
   cider vinegar

1 teaspoon dried thyme

6 (½-inch-thick) slices
   sourdough bread,
   lightly toasted

1 cup grated Gruyère cheese

1. In a large soup pot over low heat, melt the butter.
2. Add the onions and garlic and season with salt. Cook for 50 minutes, stirring occasionally, or until the onions are tender and brown.
3. Slowly stir in the vegetable broth, vinegar, and thyme. Turn the heat to medium and bring the soup to a boil. Reduce the heat to low and simmer for 10 minutes.
4. Preheat the broiler.
5. While the soup simmers, place the toasted bread slices on a baking sheet. Divide the cheese evenly among the slices and broil for about 2 minutes until the cheese melts.
6. Divide the soup evenly among bowls and top with the cheesy bread before serving.

PER SERVING: CALORIES: 256; TOTAL FAT: 12G; SATURATED FAT: 7G; CARBOHYDRATES: 26G; FIBER: 3G; PROTEIN: 9G; SODIUM: 311MG

PREP TIP: If you're short on time, you can fry the onions in a skillet over high heat for 10 minutes until golden, stirring often, but the oniony flavor won't be quite as developed.

ANDALUSIAN GAZPACHO

30 MINUTES OR LESS ✦ NUT FREE ✦ VEGAN

PREP TIME: 20 MINUTES • SERVES 6

Gazpacho is a nutritious, thirst-quenching soup that originated in the sweltering south of Spain. It is believed that gazpacho was first created when the Moors would make stale, dry bread more palatable by dipping it into chopped tomatoes. This dish can be eaten at room temperature or chilled for an hour before serving, if you really need to cool down.

2 slices slightly stale bread, crusts removed

2 small cucumbers, peeled and finely chopped, divided

1 small sweet onion, finely chopped

1 garlic clove, mashed

3 pounds ripe tomatoes, peeled, seeded, and diced, plus 1 tomato, finely diced

1 green bell pepper, seeded and diced

3 tablespoons red wine vinegar

6 tablespoons olive oil

1 teaspoon chopped fresh oregano

⅛ teaspoon salt

⅛ teaspoon freshly ground black pepper

4 scallions, white and green parts, chopped

1. In a shallow bowl, combine the bread with enough water to cover. Soak the bread for about 2 minutes until just softened. Squeeze out the excess water and place the bread in a food processor.
2. Add half the cucumbers, the onion, garlic, and diced tomatoes to the food processor. Purée until smooth and transfer to a large bowl.
3. Stir in the remaining cucumbers, green bell pepper, and vinegar.
4. In a small bowl, stir together the olive oil, finely diced tomato, oregano, salt, and pepper.
5. Divide the soup evenly among bowls and sprinkle with the tomato-pepper mixture and scallions.

PER SERVING: CALORIES: 215; TOTAL FAT: 15G; SATURATED FAT: 2G; CARBOHYDRATES: 20G; FIBER: 5G; PROTEIN: 4G; SODIUM: 111MG

VARIATION TIP: Use green tomatoes when they're in season to make a green gazpacho.

GAZPACHO BLANCO

VEGAN

PREP TIME: 20 MINUTES • CHILL TIME: 1 HOUR • SERVES 6

In earlier times, this soup was made with whatever the cook happened to have on hand, which meant none of our New World luxuries—and, of course, slightly stale bread. As such, I think this version is probably the closest to the original gazpacho recipe. The grapes add a touch of sweetness and texture.

4 small slices slightly stale bread

1 cup water

1 cup blanched almonds (see tips)

2 garlic cloves, peeled

3 tablespoons apple cider vinegar

¼ cup olive oil

4 cups ice water

Salt

Freshly ground black pepper

24 green seedless grapes, for serving

1. In a shallow bowl, combine the bread and water. Soak the bread for about 10 minutes until soft. Squeeze out the excess water and place the bread in a food processor.
2. Add the almonds and garlic and pulse until well combined. With the food processor running, slowly add the vinegar, olive oil, and ice water.
3. Process until you have a smooth white liquid. Taste and season with salt and pepper.
4. Transfer the soup to a large bowl, cover, and refrigerate to chill for at least 1 hour.
5. Serve the soup topped with the grapes.

PER SERVING: CALORIES: 272; TOTAL FAT: 22G; SATURATED FAT: 2G; CARBOHYDRATES: 15G; FIBER: 4G; PROTEIN: 8G; SODIUM: 116MG

INGREDIENT TIP: To blanch almonds, place raw almonds in boiling water and let sit for 1 minute. Drain and rinse under cold water. Gently squeeze the nuts from their skins—they should slide out.

SUBSTITUTION TIP: Use 4 cups almond milk in place of the almonds and ice water.

STONE SOUP

FREEZER FRIENDLY ✦ NUT FREE

PREP TIME: 20 MINUTES • COOK TIME: 30 MINUTES • SERVES 6

Stone soup originated from a Mediterranean folktale. The legend says a stranger travel-ing through a small town asked its residents to share one ingredient from each of their kitchens, which he then combined to make a soup to ease his hunger. In this recipe, you won't need to go door to door, just to the local grocery store or farmers' market.

8 cups vegetable broth

2 potatoes, peeled and cut into 1-inch cubes

2 celery stalks, chopped

2 cups cut green beans

1 yellow summer squash, cut into 1-inch cubes

1 carrot, cut into ½-inch slices

1 onion, chopped

1 green bell pepper, seeded and diced

¼ cup quick cooking barley

1 (16-ounce) can diced tomatoes

2 tablespoons chopped fresh oregano

⅛ teaspoon salt

⅛ teaspoon freshly ground black pepper

½ cup freshly grated Parmesan cheese (optional)

2 cups bread croutons (optional)

1. In a large soup pot over medium-high heat, combine the vegetable broth, potatoes, celery, green beans, squash, carrot, onion, and green bell pepper. Stir to combine.
2. Bring to a boil. Cover the pot, reduce the heat to low, and simmer for 10 minutes. Stir in the barley and simmer for 10 minutes more.
3. Add the tomatoes, oregano, salt, and pepper. Increase the heat to medium-high and bring the soup to a boil before reducing the heat to maintain a simmer and cook-ing for 5 minutes more.
4. Turn off the heat, let the soup rest for 5 minutes, and serve topped with the Parmesan cheese and croutons (if using).

PER SERVING: CALORIES: 128; TOTAL FAT: 0G; SATURATED FAT: 0G; CARBOHYDRATES: 26G; FIBER: 6G; PROTEIN: 3G; SODIUM: 112MG

LEFTOVERS TIP: Leftovers can be frozen for up to 1 month. To use, thaw in the refrigerator overnight. In a small pot over medium heat, combine the soup and ½ cup water. Heat until warmed through.

SUBSTITUTION TIP: Use frozen cut green beans in place of fresh beans. Thaw the beans and add them when you add the tomatoes.

TABBOULEH SALAD

30 MINUTES OR LESS ✦ NUT FREE ✦ VEGAN

PREP TIME: 20 MINUTES • SERVES 6

This side dish has long been a staple in Eastern Mediterranean countries. It's rapidly gaining popularity around the world for its fantastic mix of vitamins, minerals, fiber, antioxidants, and carbohydrates. The perfect accompaniment to Roasted Root Vegetables (page 56) or Eggplant and Lentil Tagine (page 82), this salad takes less than 30 minutes to make and tastes even better the next day when the flavors have had a chance to develop.

1 cup fine bulgur wheat

1 cup hot water

4 cups finely chopped fresh parsley

2 tomatoes, diced

1 sweet onion, chopped

½ cup olive oil

½ cup freshly squeezed lemon juice, plus more as needed

⅛ teaspoon salt, plus more as needed

1. In a medium bowl, combine the bulgur and hot water. Let sit for about 5 minutes until soft.
2. In another medium bowl, stir together the parsley, tomatoes, and onion.
3. Drain the excess water from the bulgur and add it to the tomato mixture.
4. Drizzle with the olive oil and lemon juice. Stir to combine. Sprinkle with the salt, taste, and add more salt or lemon juice, as needed.
5. Refrigerate leftovers in an airtight container for up to 1 week.

PER SERVING: CALORIES: 260; TOTAL FAT: 18G; SATURATED FAT: 3G; CARBOHYDRATES: 23G; FIBER: 5G; PROTEIN: 5G; SODIUM: 82MG

SUBSTITUTION TIP: For people allergic to gluten, replace the bulgur with cooked quinoa.

FATTOUSH

30 MINUTES OR LESS ✦ NUT FREE ✦ VEGAN

PREP TIME: 20 MINUTES • COOK TIME: 5 MINUTES • SERVES 6

Although crunchy on its own due to the cucumber, radish, and bell pepper, this salad uses toasted pita bread to make croutons for added texture and flavor. The refreshing combination of mint, tangy lemon juice, and fresh vegetables makes this salad a summer staple of Mediterranean cuisine, and I'm sure it will be a big hit at your warm-weather picnics and potlucks, too.

2 loaves slightly stale pita bread, cut into 2-inch squares

½ cup olive oil

¼ cup freshly squeezed lemon juice

2 tablespoons pomegranate molasses, or cranberry juice

1 tablespoon Sanaa's Za'atar (page 44), or store-bought

6 romaine lettuce leaves, chopped

2 tomatoes, diced

2 Persian cucumbers, diced

1 red bell pepper, seeded and diced

4 scallions, white and green parts, chopped

2 radishes, thinly sliced

1 cup chopped fresh parsley

½ cup chopped fresh mint

Salt

Freshly ground black pepper

1. Preheat the oven to 350°F.
2. Place the pita squares in a single layer on a baking sheet and toast in the oven for about 5 minutes until golden. Remove and set aside.
3. In a medium bowl, whisk the olive oil, lemon juice, molasses, and za'atar until blended. Set aside.
4. In a large bowl, combine the lettuce, tomatoes, cucumbers, red bell pepper, scallions, radishes, parsley, and mint. Drizzle with the dressing and toss well to coat. Taste and season with salt and pepper, as needed. Top with the pita chips to serve.

PER SERVING: CALORIES: 253; TOTAL FAT: 18G; SATURATED FAT: 3G; CARBOHYDRATES: 23G; FIBER: 3G; PROTEIN: 3G; SODIUM: 155MG

THE HISTORY OF ZA'ATAR

Za'atar refers to two things in Arabic: an herb (sometimes called "wild thyme") that grows, primarily, in the hills of the Eastern Mediterranean region and a condiment made with that herb combined with sumac and sesame seeds.

Long ago, women from seaside villages tried to make extra money by collecting the wild thyme, drying it in the sun, and selling it to local shops. To add color and weight to their bundles, the women added ground sumac berries, which also grow wild in the Mediterranean region. Later the spice shop owners added sesame seeds and other spices to this mixture and, thus, za'atar as we know it today was born.

While I was growing up, a za'atar wrap was my family's favorite grab-and-go snack. My mom would spread a mixture of za'atar and olive oil on a fresh pita, roll it up, and give it to us to eat while studying, or for breakfast on our way to school. It also tastes great sprinkled over Mint Labneh (page 15) or Hummus (page 10) or mixed with olive oil and used as a marinade.

Everyone has their own za'atar recipe. This is mine, but feel free to experiment! You can substitute dried oregano for the thyme, add coriander seeds, or include a pinch of red pepper flakes for an added kick.

SANAA'S ZA'ATAR

30 MINUTES OR LESS ✦ GLUTEN FREE ✦ NUT FREE ✦ VEGAN

PREP TIME: 5 MINUTES • MAKES 2¼ CUPS

1 cup dried thyme

½ cup ground sumac

½ cup sesame seeds, toasted

¼ teaspoon salt

In a small bowl, stir together the thyme, sumac, sesame seeds, and salt. Store the mixture in an airtight container in the pantry for up to 1 year.

ALMOST NIÇOISE SALAD

DAIRY FREE ✦ GLUTEN FREE ✦ NUT FREE

PREP TIME: 30 MINUTES • COOK TIME: 10 MINUTES • SERVES 4

If you were to walk along the streets of Nice, in Southern France, you would discover this salad on almost every café menu. Although the original recipe uses tuna, I think the eggs provide enough protein to keep you full and still allow the salad to pay significant homage to the classic version.

1 pound small red
  potatoes, halved

8 ounces green
  beans, trimmed

1 head Boston lettuce,
  leaves separated

4 large hardboiled eggs,
  peeled and quartered
  (see tip)

8 cherry tomatoes, halved

¼ cup white wine vinegar

3 tablespoons Dijon mustard

⅛ teaspoon salt

⅛ teaspoon freshly ground
  black pepper

¼ cup olive oil

1 cup cured black olives

1. Place the potatoes in a saucepan, cover with water, and bring to a boil over high heat. Cook for about 5 minutes until the potatoes are soft but not mushy. Drain and set aside.
2. In another saucepan over medium-high heat, heat enough water to cover the green beans until boiling. Add the green beans and cook for about 2 minutes to blanch.
3. Line shallow salad bowls with the lettuce leaves. Evenly divide the potatoes, green beans, egg quarters, and cherry tomatoes among the bowls.
4. In a small bowl, whisk the vinegar, mustard, salt, and pepper until combined. While whisking, slowly add the olive oil, until you have a well-emulsified dressing. Drizzle the dressing over the salads and top each with the olives before serving.

PER SERVING: CALORIES: 332; TOTAL FAT: 21G; SATURATED FAT: 4G; CARBOHYDRATES: 29G; FIBER: 6G; PROTEIN: 11G; SODIUM: 495MG

INGREDIENT TIP: For perfect hardboiled eggs, place the eggs in a saucepan and cover with cold water by 1 inch. Bring to a boil over medium-high heat. Cover the pan and cook for 7 minutes. Using a slotted spoon, remove the eggs from the pot, run them under cold water for 2 to 3 minutes, and peel.

MEDITERRANEAN POTATO SALAD

30 MINUTES OR LESS ✦ GLUTEN FREE ✦ NUT FREE ✦ VEGAN

PREP TIME: 15 MINUTES • COOK TIME: 15 MINUTES • SERVES 6

This potato salad is very refreshing. I make it whenever I am invited to a Fourth of July picnic; the dressing of olive oil and lemon juice makes it safe to sit on the table for hours in summer's heat—unlike the mayonnaise-loaded version. You can make this salad a day before serving and it will last a week in the refrigerator.

4 russet potatoes

1 red bell pepper, seeded and finely diced

1 red onion, finely chopped

2 cups chopped fresh parsley

½ cup capers, drained

¼ cup olive oil

¼ cup freshly squeezed lemon juice

Grated zest of 1 lemon

1 teaspoon dried thyme

⅛ teaspoon salt

1. Place the potatoes in a medium saucepan, cover with cold water, and bring to a boil over medium-high heat. Cook for about 15 minutes until the potatoes are soft but not overcooked. You want to be able to pierce them with a fork but have them stay whole. Drain and let cool.
2. Peel the potatoes and cut them into ½-inch cubes. Place the potatoes in a medium bowl.
3. Add the red bell pepper, red onion, parsley, and capers to the bowl and set aside.
4. In a small bowl, whisk the olive oil, lemon juice, lemon zest, thyme, and salt until well combined. Drizzle the dressing over the potato salad and toss until well coated. Serve chilled or at room temperature.

PER SERVING: CALORIES: 211; TOTAL FAT: 9G; SATURATED FAT: 1G; CARBOHYDRATES: 31G; FIBER: 4G; PROTEIN: 4G; SODIUM: 312MG

PANZANELLA SALAD

30 MINUTES OR LESS ✦ NUT FREE ✦ VEGAN

PREP TIME: 20 MINUTES • COOK TIME: 5 MINUTES • SERVES 6

Panzanella was originally a peasant dish derived from the need to use up stale bread. The word *panzanella* comes from two Italian words: *pane* meaning "bread," and *zanella* meaning "soup bowl." Sometimes I make individual panzanella bowls by placing a slice of olive bread in a salad bowl, topping it with chopped vegetables, and drizzling the dressing over all.

1 small loaf French bread, cut into 1-inch cubes (about 6 cups)

¼ cup olive oil, divided

3 large tomatoes

2 Persian cucumbers, cut into ½-inch-thick rounds

1 small red onion, thinly sliced

1 cup chopped fresh basil

1 garlic clove, mashed to a paste

¼ cup red wine vinegar

⅛ teaspoon salt

1. Preheat the oven to 350°F.
2. In a large bowl, toss the bread cubes with 2 tablespoons of olive oil until coated. Spread the cubes in a single layer on a baking sheet. Bake for 5 minutes or until the bread is lightly toasted. Divide the toasted cubes evenly among serving bowls.
3. Dice the tomatoes into a colander set over a bowl to collect the juices. Transfer the tomatoes to a medium bowl and set the bowl containing the juice aside.
4. Add the cucumbers, red onion, basil, and garlic to the tomatoes.
5. Add the remaining 2 tablespoons of olive oil, the vinegar, and salt to the bowl containing the tomato juice and whisk until well combined. Drizzle the dressing over the vegetables and toss well to mix.
6. Divide the vegetables and dressing among the bowls with the bread and serve.

PER SERVING: CALORIES: 348; TOTAL FAT: 18G; SATURATED FAT: 3G; CARBOHYDRATES: 41G; FIBER: 3G; PROTEIN: 8G; SODIUM: 293MG

LENTIL AND FETA SALAD

30 MINUTES OR LESS ✦ GLUTEN FREE ✦ NUT FREE

PREP TIME: 10 MINUTES • COOK TIME: 15 MINUTES • SERVES 6

How can you feed up to six people a healthy, delicious meal for only five dollars in under 20 minutes? It's easy—just make this salad! In my home, making this salad is a team effort. Because lentils don't take long to cook, I chop the vegetables while they boil and my daughter crumbles the feta. Dinner is on the table in 15 minutes, and leftovers taste even better the next day.

2 cups chopped fresh parsley

2 celery stalks, diced

2 baby cucumbers, diced

1 red onion, diced

1 yellow bell pepper, seeded and diced

¼ cup olive oil

½ cup freshly squeezed lemon juice

1 teaspoon chopped fresh oregano

1 pound dried brown lentils, rinsed and picked over for debris

8 cups water

½ cup crumbled feta cheese

1. In a large bowl, combine the parsley, celery, cucumbers, red onion, and yellow bell pepper. Set aside.
2. In a small bowl, whisk the olive oil, lemon juice, and oregano until well combined. Pour the dressing over the vegetables and toss well to coat. Set aside.
3. In a large pot over medium-high heat, combine the lentils and water. Bring to a boil. Once boiling, reduce the heat to maintain a simmer and cook for 15 minutes until the lentils are just done. Drain and add the lentils, while still hot, to the vegetables. Toss well to combine. Sprinkle with the feta cheese to serve.

PER SERVING: CALORIES: 402; TOTAL FAT: 12G; SATURATED FAT: 3G; CARBOHYDRATES: 52G; FIBER: 25G; PROTEIN: 23G; SODIUM: 165MG

LEFTOVERS TIP: Refrigerated in an airtight container, this salad will last up to 1 week. Bring it to room temperature for 30 minutes before serving to bring out the flavors.

GREEK SALAD

30 MINUTES OR LESS ✦ GLUTEN FREE ✦ NUT FREE

PREP TIME: 20 MINUTES • SERVES 6

This salad is perfect for potlucks and neighborhood parties. Greek salad purists insist this salad should be made only with diced cucumber, diced tomato, chopped onion, olives, and feta. But I have made it with romaine lettuce, pickled artichoke hearts, pickled peppers, and even diced raw zucchini. The rich flavors of the olives and feta cheese make it pleasing to everyone and very filling. You only need add a slice of good bread for a great meal.

10 romaine lettuce leaves, chopped

1 red onion, thinly sliced

1 green bell pepper, seeded and chopped

2 large tomatoes, diced

2 Persian cucumbers, cut into slices

1 cup pitted Kalamata olives

¼ cup chopped fresh oregano

6 tablespoons olive oil

¼ cup freshly squeezed lemon juice

1 cup crumbled feta cheese

1. In a large salad bowl, combine the lettuce leaves, red onion, green bell pepper, tomatoes, cucumbers, olives, and oregano. Toss until well mixed. Set aside.
2. In a small bowl, whisk the olive oil and lemon juice until blended. Pour the dressing over the salad and toss well to coat.
3. Sprinkle with the feta cheese to serve.

PER SERVING: CALORIES: 264; TOTAL FAT: 22G; SATURATED FAT: 6G; CARBOHYDRATES: 14G; FIBER: 4G; PROTEIN: 6G; SODIUM: 342MG

INGREDIENT TIP: Taste this salad before adding any salt, as feta cheese is very salty on its own.

SHEPHERD'S SALAD

30 MINUTES OR LESS ✦ GLUTEN FREE ✦ NUT FREE

PREP TIME: 15 MINUTES • SERVES 6

A traditional side across much of Turkey, shepherd's salad has become a vegetarian favorite. Filled with delicious fresh produce and bursting with flavor and color, it is sure to brighten any table and many a face. The salad's name derives from a long history of shepherds returning to their farms having collected fresh produce along the way, which they then used to make this delicious and vibrant classic.

4 large ripe tomatoes, diced

4 Persian cucumbers, diced

6 scallions, white and green parts, chopped

1 green bell pepper, seeded and chopped

1 cup crumbled feta cheese (optional)

½ cup chopped fresh parsley

¼ cup olive oil

3 tablespoons red wine vinegar

⅛ teaspoon salt

⅛ teaspoon freshly ground black pepper

1. In a large salad bowl, combine the tomatoes, cucumbers, scallions, green bell pepper, feta cheese (if using), and parsley. Set aside.
2. In a small bowl, whisk the olive oil, vinegar, salt, and pepper until combined. Drizzle the dressing over the vegetables and toss well to coat.

PER SERVING: CALORIES: 139; TOTAL FAT: 9G; SATURATED FAT: 1G; CARBOHYDRATES: 15G; FIBER: 3G; PROTEIN: 3G; SODIUM: 66MG

GOAT CHEESE AND ARUGULA SANDWICH

30 MINUTES OR LESS ✦ NUT FREE

PREP TIME: 15 MINUTES • SERVES 1

Arugula, called *roquette* in French, has a slightly spicy, nutty taste. It's a great addition to sandwiches and salads and, in this recipe, is a wonderful complement to the creamy goat cheese and salty olives. Feel free to experiment with additional toppings: My husband loves raw sweet onion with his, and my daughter sprinkles the cheese with za'atar before adding the arugula. I love to use my panini press to make this sandwich; if you don't have one, toasting the sandwich in the oven for a few minutes will do the trick.

2 ounces soft goat cheese

1 tablespoon olive oil

1 teaspoon black olive paste (see tip)

2 slices sourdough bread

¼ cup arugula leaves

1. In a small bowl, stir together the goat cheese, olive oil, and olive paste until well combined.
2. Spread this mixture over one bread slice. Top with the arugula, cover with other slice of bread, and enjoy.

PER SERVING: CALORIES: 404; TOTAL FAT: 28G; SATURATED FAT: 11G; CARBOHYDRATES: 24G; FIBER: 1G; PROTEIN: 15G; SODIUM: 450MG

SUBSTITUTION TIP: If you can't find olive paste, use Green Olive Tapenade (page 13), or chop a few pitted black or Kalamata olives instead.

FALAFEL SANDWICH

30 MINUTES OR LESS ✦ NUT FREE ✦ VEGAN

PREP TIME: 15 MINUTES • COOK TIME: 15 MINUTES • SERVES 4

In elementary school in Syria, I would buy a falafel sandwich on the way home and then proclaim I had no appetite when my mother offered her home-cooked meal. Although originally a simple street food, falafel has rapidly expanded in popularity—and it is likely responsible for spoiling dinner plans around the globe. I've included my favorite toppings here, but you could add pickles, Tzatziki Sauce (page 144), olives, or anything else your heart desires.

2 tomatoes, diced

1 cup chopped lettuce

1 cucumber, diced

1 cup Pickled Turnips (page 19), chopped (optional)

⅛ teaspoon salt

2 cups corn oil, or vegetable oil

2 cups Homemade Falafel Mix (page 154), or store-bought, formed into 2-inch balls

6 Pita Bread loaves (page 152), or store-bought

6 tablespoons Hummus (page 10), or store-bought, divided

1 cup Tahini Sauce (page 140)

1. Line a plate with paper towels and set aside.
2. In a medium bowl, gently stir together the tomatoes, lettuce, cucumber, turnips (if using), and salt. Set aside.
3. In a sauté pan or skillet over medium heat, heat the corn oil until it reaches 375°F. You can use a digital thermometer or a small falafel ball to test the temperature—if the falafel sizzles immediately when dropped into the hot oil, it's ready to cook.
4. Gently add the falafel balls to the hot oil and fry them until golden brown on both sides, about 2 to 3 minutes per side. Using a slotted spoon, transfer the falafel to the prepared plate to drain.
5. Open each pita bread and spread 1 tablespoon of hummus inside. Spoon the vegetable mixture over the hummus, add a couple falafel balls, drizzle with tahini sauce, and enjoy.

PER SERVING: (4 BALLS) CALORIES: 614; TOTAL FAT: 28G; SATURATED FAT: 3G; CARBOHYDRATES: 77G; FIBER: 17G; PROTEIN: 21G; SODIUM: 493MG

PREP TIP: Moisten the falafel with olive oil and bake them in a 375°F oven for 10 minutes or until golden brown, for a healthier option.

CAPRESE SANDWICH

30 MINUTES OR LESS

PREP TIME: 15 MINUTES • SERVES 1

Although thought to have originated on the Italian isle of Capri, and so named, there is no way to know for sure where this flavorful vegetarian sandwich came from. One thing that is sure, though: There's really nothing quite like a fresh caprese sandwich, with its herbaceous basil, salty mozzarella, and juicy tomatoes—delicious any time of day. I like my caprese sandwiches toasted, which adds a layer of texture. Here I use a toaster, but you can use a panini press if available, or place the sandwich on a baking sheet and heat in a 350°F oven for 5 minutes or until crispy and golden.

2 slices Italian bread

1 teaspoon Basil Pesto (page 141), or store-bought

2 (¼-inch-thick) slices fresh mozzarella cheese

1 ripe tomato, cut into ½-inch-thick slices

¼ cup chopped fresh basil

⅛ teaspoon salt

⅛ teaspoon freshly ground black pepper

1. Toast the bread until lightly golden.
2. Spread ½ teaspoon of pesto on each piece of toast and place the mozzarella slices on one piece.
3. Top the cheese with the tomato and basil. Sprinkle with the salt and pepper. Top with the other piece of toast and serve.

PER SERVING: CALORIES: 345; TOTAL FAT: 18G; SATURATED FAT: 9G; CARBOHYDRATES: 27G; FIBER: 3G; PROTEIN: 19G; SODIUM: 613MG

VARIATION TIP: This sandwich tastes great with roasted red peppers as well.

CHAPTER 4
MEATLESS MAINS

ROASTED ROOT VEGETABLES

GLUTEN FREE ✦ NUT FREE ✦ VEGAN

PREP TIME: 20 MINUTES • COOK TIME: 40 MINUTES • SERVES 6

The spices define this dish—transforming the vegetables from a light snack into a delicious main course. If you change the spices to thyme, oregano, and basil, you can create an Italian-inspired take. Experiment and find your favorite combination.

2 red onions, quartered

2 potatoes, peeled and cut into 2-inch cubes

2 red bell peppers, seeded and cut into 1-inch strips

2 zucchini, cut into 2-inch sticks

1 sweet potato, peeled and cut into 2-inch cubes

¼ cup olive oil

2 garlic cloves, mashed

2 teaspoons ground coriander

1 teaspoon salt

1 teaspoon sweet paprika

½ teaspoon ground cumin

1 tablespoon chopped fresh cilantro

2 tablespoons freshly squeezed lime juice

1. Preheat the oven to 375°F.
2. In a large bowl, combine the red onions, potatoes, red bell peppers, zucchini, and sweet potato. Set aside.
3. In a small bowl, whisk the olive oil, garlic, coriander, salt, paprika, and cumin until well combined.
4. Pour the olive oil mixture over the vegetables and toss well to coat.
5. Arrange the vegetables on a baking sheet (see tip) in a single layer. Roast for about 40 minutes until tender.
6. Sprinkle with the cilantro and drizzle with the lime juice.

PER SERVING: CALORIES: 179; TOTAL FAT: 9G; SATURATED FAT: 1G; CARBOHYDRATES: 24G; FIBER: 5G; PROTEIN: 3G; SODIUM: 333MG

COOKING TIP: Do not crowd the vegetables on the pan. Divide them between two baking sheets, if needed, so they cook evenly and roast, not steam.

STUFFED POTATOES

GLUTEN FREE ✦ VEGAN

PREP TIME: 20 MINUTES • COOK TIME: 55 MINUTES • SERVES 4

It's no secret that Mediterranean cooking has a love of stuffed vegetables. Here I stuff the humble potato to take it from side dish to main dish. My mother would cut the potatoes in half, top them with the stuffing, pour the sauce over, and bake. Feel free to try her version if you're short on time.

¼ cup olive oil

1 onion, chopped

1 pound white mushrooms, finely chopped

¼ cup pine nuts

¼ teaspoon ground cumin

¼ teaspoon ground coriander

¼ teaspoon ground allspice

⅜ teaspoon salt, divided

8 Yukon Gold potatoes, peeled

4 cups crushed tomatoes

2 cups water

2 garlic cloves, minced

⅛ teaspoon freshly ground black pepper

PREP TIP: If you do not have a vegetable corer, blanch the potatoes by dropping them into boiling water for 5 minutes. Remove and use a teaspoon to carve out the potatoes for the stuffing.

1. Preheat the oven to 375°F.
2. In a medium saucepan over medium heat, heat the olive oil.
3. Add the onion and sauté for 2 to 3 minutes.
4. Add the mushrooms and cook for about 10 minutes until their water evaporates.
5. Stir in the pine nuts, cumin, coriander, allspice, and ¼ teaspoon of salt. Set aside.
6. Using a vegetable corer, carve out the middle of each potato until the potatoes look like cups.
7. Spoon the mushroom stuffing into the cavities, filling each. Place the potatoes in a single layer, stuffing-side up, on a rimmed baking sheet. Set aside.
8. In a small bowl, stir together the tomatoes, water, garlic, remaining ⅛ teaspoon of salt, and the pepper. Pour the tomato mixture over the potatoes. Cover the baking sheet with aluminum foil.
9. Bake for 40 minutes until the stuffing is hot and the potatoes are fork-tender.

PER SERVING: CALORIES: 706; TOTAL FAT: 32G; SATURATED FAT: 4G; CARBOHYDRATES: 95G; FIBER: 20G; PROTEIN: 18G; SODIUM: 461MG

STUFFED ARTICHOKE HEARTS

GLUTEN FREE ✦ NUT FREE ✦ VEGAN

PREP TIME: 15 MINUTES • COOK TIME: 35 MINUTES • SERVES 4

In Damascus, where I'm from, there is a street called Street of the Lazy. It is called this because you can find bags of chopped parsley ready for tabbouleh, hollowed zucchini all set for stuffing, and artichoke bottoms ready to be cooked. My mother thought it all was a waste of money—except when it came to the artichokes; she hated cleaning artichokes. I won't judge you if you buy your artichokes already prepared for filling. You can find them in the frozen section of the grocery store (make sure to thaw them before using), though I promise that fresh artichokes aren't too hard to clean—and the result is delicious no matter how you get there.

FOR THE ARTICHOKES

8 cups water

10 artichokes, stemmed and cored

FOR THE STUFFING

¼ cup olive oil

1 small onion, chopped

1 cup fresh peas

1 carrot, peeled and diced

1 cup basmati rice

½ teaspoon ground turmeric

⅛ teaspoon salt

⅛ teaspoon freshly ground black pepper

TO MAKE THE ARTICHOKES

In a large pot over medium-high heat, bring the water to a boil. Gently drop the artichokes into the boiling water and cook for about 5 minutes until tender. Drain and arrange the artichokes on a serving platter.

TO MAKE THE STUFFING

1. In a medium saucepan over medium heat, heat the olive oil. Add the onion and cook for 2 to 3 minutes until golden.

2. Add the peas and carrot and cook for 5 minutes more, stirring occasionally.

3. Stir in the rice, turmeric, salt, and pepper. Increase the heat to bring the mixture to a boil. Reduce the heat to low, cover the pan, and cook for 15 minutes. Remove from the heat and let rest, covered, for 10 minutes.

FOR THE SAUCE

2 tablespoons cornstarch

2 cups water

2 garlic cloves, minced

½ teaspoon grated peeled fresh ginger

¼ teaspoon white pepper

¼ teaspoon grated nutmeg

⅛ teaspoon salt

TO MAKE THE SAUCE

1. In a small bowl, whisk the cornstarch and water until the cornstarch dissolves. Transfer to a medium saucepan and place it over medium-low heat.
2. Add the garlic, ginger, white pepper, nutmeg, and salt. Cook for 5 to 8 minutes, stirring constantly, until the sauce thickens. Remove from the heat.

TO STUFF THE ARTICHOKES

Stuff each artichoke with the rice filling and drizzle each with the sauce. Serve any remaining rice alongside the stuffed artichokes.

PER SERVING: CALORIES: 502; TOTAL FAT: 15G; SATURATED FAT: 2G; CARBOHYDRATES: 84G; FIBER: 20G; PROTEIN: 16G; SODIUM: 432MG

STUFFED ZUCCHINI

FREEZER FRIENDLY ✦ GLUTEN FREE ✦ NUT FREE

PREP TIME: 20 MINUTES • COOK TIME: 1 HOUR, 5 MINUTES • SERVES 4

When I asked my grandmother why she undertook such a time-consuming task as stuffing vegetables, her response was that stuffed vegetables were more interesting, more filling, and make a tasty main course out of simple ingredients. She stuffed grape leaves, cabbage leaves, zucchini, squash, potatoes, eggplant, and artichokes—and it is some of her recipes I am passing along to you to enjoy. This one is a special favorite.

6 zucchini, halved lengthwise

¼ cup olive oil

1 onion, chopped

2 cups chopped white mushrooms

1 green bell pepper, seeded and diced

4 garlic cloves, crushed

2 cups cooked lentils

1 (15-ounce) can diced tomatoes

2 tablespoons tomato paste

2 tablespoons pomegranate molasses, or cranberry juice

1 tablespoon Harissa (page 143), or store-bought

1. Preheat the oven to 375°F.
2. Heat a medium pot full of water over medium heat for 10 minutes. Add the zucchini and cook for 2 to 3 minutes to blanch. Using tongs, remove the zucchini from the water and let cool.
3. Using a teaspoon, scoop out the seeds from the zucchini halves to create a cavity for the stuffing. Discard the pulp. Arrange the zucchini halves in a 9-by-13-inch baking dish, cut-side up, and set aside.
4. In a skillet over medium heat, heat the olive oil. Add the onion and cook for about 8 minutes until golden.
5. Stir in the mushrooms, green bell pepper, and garlic. Cook for 5 minutes. Stir in the cooked lentils, tomatoes, tomato paste, molasses, harissa, water, salt, and pepper. Cover the skillet and cook for 5 minutes. Taste and season with more salt and pepper, as needed.

½ cup water

⅛ teaspoon salt, plus more
as needed

⅛ teaspoon freshly ground
black pepper, plus more
as needed

½ cup feta cheese (optional)

Tzatziki Sauce (page 144), for
serving (optional)

6. Fill the cavity of each zucchini with the lentil mixture and spoon any remaining sauce in the skillet over the zucchini. Cover the baking dish with aluminum foil.
7. Bake for 20 minutes. Remove the foil, sprinkle the feta cheese on top (if using), and bake for 10 minutes more or until golden brown.
8. Serve topped with tzatziki (if using).

PER SERVING: CALORIES: 343; TOTAL FAT: 15G; SATURATED FAT: 2G; CARBOHYDRATES: 44G; FIBER: G14; PROTEIN: 16G; SODIUM: 168MG

MAKE AHEAD: Prepare the recipe through step 6. Freeze the wrapped baking dish for up to 4 weeks. When ready to bake, remove from the freezer and bake, covered, in a 375°F oven for 30 minutes. Remove the foil, sprinkle on the feta (if using) and bake for 10 minutes more or until cooked through.

STUFFED CABBAGE

GLUTEN FREE ✦ VEGAN

PREP TIME: 40 MINUTES • COOKING TIME: 1 HOUR, 5 MINUTES • SERVES 6

This dish is full of nostalgia for me. While growing up, my siblings and I loved stuffed cabbage leaves. Each of us would eat at least a dozen stuffed leaves in one sitting. My mother would spend hours stuffing cabbage leaves for a meal we would finish in minutes. When we were older, she made us join her in stuffing the cabbage and we had so much fun working and teasing each other when we would mess up. And, of course, we took all the credit when the meal turned out delicious.

4 tablespoons olive oil, divided

1 small onion, chopped

2 cups short-grain rice

4 cups water, plus more for cooking the cabbage

4 garlic cloves, minced

½ teaspoon dried sage

½ teaspoon crumbled dried rosemary

2 tablespoons pine nuts

1 large head cabbage, cored

1 (28-ounce) can crushed tomatoes

¼ cup chopped olives

1 tablespoon chopped fresh rosemary

1. Preheat the oven to 375°F. Line a large plate with a clean kitchen towel and set aside.
2. In a medium pot over medium heat, heat 2 tablespoons of olive oil. Add the onion and cook for 5 minutes.
3. Add the rice and water. Increase the heat and bring the liquid to a boil. Reduce the heat to low, cover the pot, and cook for 10 minutes until the water is absorbed.
4. Transfer the rice to a medium bowl. Add the garlic, sage, dried rosemary, and pine nuts. Toss well to combine and set aside.
5. Bring a large pot of water to a boil over high heat. Gently drop the cabbage into the boiling water. Cook for 5 minutes.
6. Using long, sturdy tongs, gently transfer the cabbage to the prepared plate to drain excess water. Remove the outer leaves of the cabbage; you'll need about 16 leaves.

7. Place a cabbage leaf on a flat surface. Remove the thick stem in the center but keep the leaf intact. Place about ¼ cup of the stuffing in the center. Fold the sides over the filling and roll up the leaf. Place the stuffed leaf, seam-side down, in a 9-by-13-inch baking dish. Repeat until you finish stuffing all the leaves.
8. In a medium bowl, stir together the tomatoes, remaining 2 tablespoons of olive oil, the olives, and fresh rosemary. Pour the sauce over the cabbage leaves.
9. Bake, uncovered, for 45 minutes. Serve immediately.

PER SERVING: CALORIES: 498; TOTAL FAT: 17G; SATURATED FAT: 2G; CARBOHYDRATES: 78G; FIBER: 12G; PROTEIN: 11G; SODIUM: 346MG

POMMES ANNA

GLUTEN FREE ✦ NUT FREE

PREP TIME: 20 MINUTES • COOK TIME: 50 MINUTES • SERVES 8

This golden cake-like potato dish was created during Napoleon III's era and named after one of the women in his court. It tastes heavenly—it is potatoes with butter (a lot), after all. I serve it with Garlic Aioli (page 142) and fresh tomato slices. When, on rare occasion, I have leftovers, I toast two slices of sourdough bread and layer the potatoes, tomatoes, and chopped scallion between the bread and savor a fantastic sandwich.

8 russet potatoes, peeled

8 tablespoons (1 stick) butter, melted, divided

1 teaspoon salt

½ teaspoon freshly ground black pepper

1. Preheat the oven to 450°F.
2. Using a mandoline or a very sharp knife, carefully cut the potatoes into uniform ⅛-inch-thick slices.
3. Generously brush the bottom of a 10-inch round oven-proof sauté pan or skillet with butter. Starting in the center of the pan, arrange the potato slices, slightly overlapping them, in a circle until you cover the bottom of the pan. Brush the potatoes with butter, sprinkle with salt and pepper, and repeat until you have used all the potatoes. Drizzle any remaining butter over the top.
4. Cover the pan with aluminum foil. Bake for 40 minutes. Remove the foil and bake for 10 minutes more.
5. Remove the pan from the oven. Using a thin spatula, loosen the edges and the bottom of the potatoes. Gently invert the potatoes onto a flat plate and serve.

PER SERVING: CALORIES: 270; TOTAL FAT: 12G; SATURATED FAT: 7G; CARBOHYDRATES: 39G; FIBER: 3G; PROTEIN: 5G; SODIUM: 326MG

PREP TIP: Do not wash the potato slices in water. The starch helps the slices stick to each other.

SPANAKOPITA

NUT FREE

PREP TIME: 20 MINUTES • COOK TIME: 50 MINUTES • SERVES 6

Today, spanakopita is usually made with filo dough or puff pastry, but it was originally made with pita dough, which is how it got its name. If you'd like to take a more traditional route, use the Pita Bread dough (page 152) to prepare this. Whatever you use, the classic combination of spinach, salty feta, and a flaky crust is always great.

1 (16-ounce) package frozen chopped spinach, thawed

¼ cup olive oil

1 onion, chopped

3 cups crumbled feta cheese

⅛ teaspoon freshly ground black pepper

All-purpose flour, for dusting

1 sheet puff pastry

1 large egg

1 tablespoon water

1 tablespoon sesame seeds

1. Preheat the oven to 400°F.
2. Using your hands, squeeze the spinach dry, or place it in a colander and press on it with a spoon to remove excess water. Set aside.
3. In a skillet over medium heat, heat the olive oil. Add the onion and cook for 5 minutes or until soft and translucent. Add the spinach and cook for 2 to 3 minutes more. Remove from the heat.
4. Stir in the feta cheese and pepper until well mixed. Spoon the spinach mixture into a 9-by-13-inch baking dish, if not using an oven-safe skillet. Set aside.
5. Dust a work surface with flour and roll out the puff pastry on it until it is the same size as the baking vessel. Gently cover the spinach mixture with the puff pastry.
6. In a small bowl, whisk the egg and water until blended. Brush the puff pastry with the egg wash. Sprinkle with the sesame seeds and cut the puff pastry into 2-inch squares.
7. Bake for about 40 minutes until golden.

PER SERVING: CALORIES: 522; TOTAL FAT: 41G; SATURATED FAT: 16G; CARBOHYDRATES: 25G; FIBER: 3G; PROTEIN: 17G; SODIUM: 912MG

SUBSTITUTION TIP: Use 6 filo dough sheets to top the spinach for a flakier crust. Melt 3 tablespoons butter and brush each sheet with it before layering. Follow the remaining instructions as written.

CHICKPEA FATAT

30 MINUTES OR LESS

PREP TIME: 10 MINUTES • COOK TIME: 15 MINUTES • SERVES 6

Walking around Damascus you will find many shops that each sells their own version of fatat. *Fatat* means "to crumble" in Arabic, and that is the idea behind this dish. Bread that is a little dry is crumbled and then topped with a variety of ingredients. This dish is usually served as a weekend breakfast dish.

3 (9-inch) day-old Pita Breads (page 152), or store-bought, cut into 1-inch squares

3 cups Plain Yogurt (page 150), or store-bought

1 cup tahini

½ cup freshly squeezed lemon juice

4 garlic cloves, crushed or mashed into a paste

1 teaspoon ground cumin

Salt

2 (15-ounce) cans chickpeas, undrained

2 tablespoons Ghee (page 148), or store-bought

¼ cup pine nuts

2 tablespoons chopped fresh parsley

1. In a deep serving platter, arrange the bread pieces in an even layer. Set aside.
2. In a large bowl, whisk the yogurt, tahini, lemon juice, garlic, and cumin until smooth. Season with salt and whisk to combine. Set aside.
3. Pour the chickpeas and their liquid into a saucepan and bring to a boil over medium-high heat. Reduce the heat to maintain a simmer and cook for about 10 minutes until the chickpeas are hot.
4. Spoon the hot chickpeas and liquid evenly over the bread. Pour the yogurt sauce over the chickpeas. Set aside.
5. In a small saucepan over medium heat, melt the ghee. Add the pine nuts. Increase the heat to medium-high and fry the nuts for about 1 minute or until slightly golden.
6. Pour the pine nuts and ghee over the yogurt sauce. Sprinkle with the parsley and serve.

PER SERVING: CALORIES: 644; TOTAL FAT: 35G; SATURATED FAT: 6G; CARBOHYDRATES: 61G; FIBER: 11G; PROTEIN: 25G; SODIUM: 289MG

SUBSTITUTION TIP: Skip the yogurt and ghee for a vegan version.

SPINACH AND RICOTTA DUMPLINGS

NUT FREE

PREP TIME: 30 MINUTES • CHILL TIME: 10 MINUTES • COOK TIME: 5 MINUTES • SERVES 4

Although there's no proof that spinach will make you as strong as Popeye, it will certainly help lower bad protein levels in the blood and protect from heart disease. Here, this powerhouse green is combined with creamy ricotta and made into delicious dumplings. These taste amazing topped with my Basic Tomato Basil Sauce (page 145) or Basil Pesto (page 141), or even just use a drizzle of good olive oil and a sprinkle of salt and freshly ground black pepper.

½ cup all-purpose flour, plus more for dusting

1 (10-ounce) package frozen chopped spinach, thawed

1 large egg

2 cups whole-milk ricotta

⅛ teaspoon freshly grated nutmeg

⅛ teaspoon salt, plus more for the cooking water

⅛ teaspoon freshly ground black pepper

Freshly grated Parmesan cheese, for serving

1. Dust a baking sheet with flour.
2. Using your hands, squeeze the spinach dry, or place it in a colander and press on it with a spoon to remove excess water. Finely chop the spinach and place it in a large bowl. Add the egg, ricotta, nutmeg, flour, salt, and pepper. Mix until well combined.
3. Dust your palms with flour to prevent the dough from sticking. Take about ¼ cup of the spinach mixture and roll it into a 2-inch ball. Place it on the prepared baking sheet. Repeat with the remaining dough, dusting your palms as needed. This should make about 20 dumplings. Refrigerate the dumplings for at least 10 minutes before cooking.
4. Bring a large pot of salted water to a boil over high heat. Lower the heat to medium and gently drop the dumplings into the water. Cook for about 5 minutes until the dumplings float to the top. Using a slotted spoon, transfer the dumplings to a plate.
5. Serve topped with your favorite sauce and a sprinkle of Parmesan cheese.

PER SERVING: CALORIES: 325; TOTAL FAT: 18G; SATURATED FAT: 10G; CARBOHYDRATES: 22G; FIBER: 2G; PROTEIN: 19G; SODIUM: 381MG

WALNUT AND POTATO DUMPLINGS WITH SPICY POMEGRANATE SAUCE

FREEZER FRIENDLY ✦ VEGAN

PREP TIME: 20 MINUTES • COOK TIME: 1 HOUR, 30 MINUTES • SERVES 6

Traditionally called *kibbeh*, this potato dumpling dish is usually made with a meat-and-pine-nut filling. In this recipe I mix walnuts with smoky cumin and onion to provide protein and a wonderful, almost meaty, texture. Although this recipe might look complicated, it comes together easily!

FOR THE SAUCE

¼ cup olive oil

1 teaspoon pomegranate molasses, or cranberry juice

1 teaspoon Harissa (page 143), or store-bought

½ teaspoon ground coriander

FOR THE STUFFING

¼ cup olive oil

3 onions, finely chopped

2 cups coarsely chopped walnuts

1 garlic clove, minced

1 teaspoon ground cumin

1 teaspoon ground coriander

⅛ teaspoon salt

TO MAKE THE SAUCE

In a small bowl, whisk the olive oil, molasses, harissa, and coriander until blended. Set aside.

TO MAKE THE STUFFING

1. In a saucepan over medium heat, heat the olive oil. Add the onions and cook for 5 minutes.
2. Add the walnuts and cook for 5 minutes more. Remove from the heat. Stir in the garlic, cumin, coriander, and salt. Set aside.

TO MAKE THE DOUGH

1. Place a large glass bowl in the refrigerator to chill.
2. In a large pot, combine the potatoes and enough water to cover by 1 inch. Place the pot over medium-high heat and bring to a boil. Reduce the heat to maintain a rolling boil and cook the potatoes for about 30 minutes until soft. Drain and let cool slightly. When the potatoes are cool enough to handle, peel and quarter them.
3. While the potatoes cook, in a small bowl, combine the bulgur and cold water and let sit for about 10 minutes until soft. Drain and squeeze out any excess water. Set aside.

FOR THE DOUGH

2 russet potatoes

4 cups fine bulgur

6 cups cold water

1 onion, quartered

½ cup pumpkin purée

½ cup whole-wheat flour

1 teaspoon ground cumin

Olive oil, for handling
   the dough

4. In a food processor, combine a quarter of the onion and a quarter of the soaked bulgur. Process for 30 seconds.

5. Add a couple potato quarters and continue to process until the mixture starts to pull away from the walls of the food processor. Transfer to the chilled bowl. Repeat the process with the remaining onion, bulgur, and potatoes.

6. Add the pumpkin to the bulgur dough, sprinkle with the flour, and add the cumin. Knead the dough until mixed well.

7. Preheat the oven to 400°F. Line a baking sheet with parchment paper.

8. Coat your palms with a bit of olive oil and portion the dough into 12 balls.

9. Place 6 dough balls on the prepared baking sheet, about 5 inches apart. Flatten the balls into ⅛-inch-thick rounds. Spoon the walnut stuffing onto each round.

10. Flatten each of the remaining 6 balls in your palm and gently place them over the stuffing. Gently seal the edges and try, using your palms, to create a dome shape.

11. Bake for 45 minutes. Drizzle with the pomegranate sauce and serve.

PER SERVING: CALORIES: 787; TOTAL FAT: 36G; SATURATED FAT: 5G; CARBOHYDRATES: 103G; FIBER: 23G; PROTEIN: 20G; SODIUM: 74MG

MAKE AHEAD: You can freeze unbaked kibbeh for up to 1 month. Place the domes on a baking sheet, cover well with aluminum foil, and freeze. When ready to bake, remove the foil and bake in a 400°F oven for 1 hour from frozen. You can also freeze the baked kibbeh in an airtight container for up to 2 months.

EGGPLANT KUFTA

VEGAN

PREP TIME: 15 MINUTES • COOK TIME: 30 MINUTES • SERVES 4

Kufta translates to "meatball" or "pounded meat." A favorite in many Mediterranean countries, you can find different regional variations, including *kofta* in Lebanon and *kefta* in Greece. My take on these savory little bites uses roasted eggplant and chopped walnuts in place of meat, lending plenty of protein to keep you full. To serve, cut a couple onions into thin slices, sprinkle them with sumac, and massage for a few minutes until softened a bit. Serve the kufta over the onions with Plain Yogurt (page 150).

1 large eggplant, cut into 2-inch cubes

¼ cup olive oil, divided

1 small onion, chopped

½ cup chopped fresh parsley

¼ cup chopped fresh cilantro

2 garlic cloves, minced

1 teaspoon sweet paprika

½ teaspoon ground coriander

¼ teaspoon cayenne pepper

⅛ teaspoon salt, plus more as needed

½ cup coarsely chopped almonds

2 cups bread crumbs

1. Preheat the broiler.
2. In a large bowl, combine the eggplant and 2 tablespoons of olive oil. Toss well to coat. Spread the eggplant on a baking sheet. Broil for about 5 minutes until golden. Remove and let cool.
3. Reduce the oven temperature to 400°F.
4. Transfer the cooled eggplant to a food processor and purée. Transfer the eggplant purée to a medium bowl.
5. In the food processor, combine the onion, parsley, and cilantro. Purée. Add this herb mixture to the eggplant, along with the garlic, paprika, coriander, cayenne, salt, almonds, and bread crumbs. Stir until well combined. Taste and season with more salt, as needed.
6. Moisten your palms with the remaining 2 tablespoons of olive oil. Form the eggplant mixture into 3-inch balls and place them on a baking sheet. You should have about 20 balls.
7. Bake for 20 minutes. Flip the balls and bake for 5 minutes more until firm.

PER SERVING: CALORIES: 478; TOTAL FAT: 24G; SATURATED FAT: 3G; CARBOHYDRATES: 56G; FIBER: 10G; PROTEIN: 13G; SODIUM: 213MG

BELL PEPPER AND ONION TART

FREEZER FRIENDLY ✦ NUT FREE

PREP TIME: 15 MINUTES • COOK TIME: 40 MINUTES • SERVES 6

This recipe is endlessly customizable. I use sweet bell peppers and onions, but experiment with whatever is in season. What I love about this dish is that it transforms simple ingredients into a delicious dinner. Sometimes, if I don't have piecrust, I make this dish and tell my family I made a crustless cheese tart—they never seem to mind!

2 tablespoons olive oil

1 red onion, chopped

All-purpose flour, for dusting

1 refrigerated
   store-bought piecrust

1 cup ricotta

½ cup heavy cream

2 large eggs

¼ cup chopped fresh basil

⅛ teaspoon salt

⅛ teaspoon freshly ground
   black pepper

2 red bell peppers, seeded and
   thinly sliced

1. Preheat the oven to 425°F.
2. In a skillet over medium heat, heat the olive oil. Add the red onion and cook for 10 minutes or until softened.
3. Dust a work surface with flour and place the crust on it. Let the crust sit for 10 minutes. Transfer the crust, flour-side down, to a 9-inch tart pan. Gently push the crust against the edges.
4. Pierce the bottom of the crust in a few places with a fork and bake for 10 minutes. Remove and set aside to cool.
5. In a medium bowl, stir together the ricotta, heavy cream, eggs, basil, salt, and pepper. Set aside.
6. Spoon the cooked onion onto the baked piecrust. Spoon the cheese mixture over the onion and arrange the red bell peppers over the cheese.
7. Bake for about 20 minutes or until the filling is set.

PER SERVING: CALORIES: 315; TOTAL FAT: 24G; SATURATED FAT: 9G; CARBOHYDRATES: 18G; FIBER: 1G; PROTEIN: 9G; SODIUM: 268MG

MAKE AHEAD: Prepare the crust and vegetables a couple days ahead and assemble the tart the day you are ready to bake it.

OLIVE OIL 101

As mentioned earlier, nothing defines Mediterranean cuisine quite like olive oil. It's the base of almost every dish, and as such, Mediterranean people take their olive oil very seriously. Every country claims their olive oil is the best in the region, and villages bicker over whose tastes better. Following are answers to some basic olive oil questions to help you get the most out of the Mediterranean's favorite ingredient.

How is it made? Olive oil has been produced the same way for thousands of years. The olives are freshly picked off the olive trees, washed, and crushed to form a paste. The paste is stirred to release the oil in a process called "maceration." No heating or chemicals—it's that simple!

How does olive oil differ by region? Italian olive oil is likely what you'll find on the shelf at your local grocery store. Olive oil from the mainland has a bold, strong flavor, whereas oil from Sicily is lighter and slightly fruitier. Olive oil from Portugal and Spain is golden in color and is lighter and fruitier in flavor than its Italian counterpart. It can even have floral notes. Greek olive oil is darker in color and has an earthy, herb-like taste. Olive oil from Eastern Mediterranean countries, such as Turkey, Syria, and Lebanon, is bold and smooth, and has a slight nutty taste. The most mildly flavored olive oil hails from France and is pale in color.

What's the difference between extra-virgin olive oil and regular olive oil? Extra-virgin olive oil is certified to be made from pure, cold-pressed olives. It's a time-consuming process, which is why it usually has a higher price point. When an oil doesn't meet EVOO-certified standards, it is processed to refine impurities, which results in a less robust flavor and lighter color. This oil is then blended with a bit of premium EVOO to produce regular olive oil.

What are some shopping and storage tips? Avoid buying olive oil bottled in clear glass bottles. Light is the enemy of olive oil and will speed its spoilage. Check for a "harvest date" within the last year or "best by" date more than a year away. You can store unopened olive oil in a cool, dark place for a couple of years but, once opened, it should be used within a few months.

How can I tell if my olive oil has gone bad? Your nose is the best indicator of quality. Good olive oil should smell like olives and have an earthy or floral aroma. When your oil has gone rancid, it has a musty smell reminiscent of cardboard, or the sharp tang of vinegar.

CHAKCHOUKA

DAIRY FREE ✦ GLUTEN FREE ✦ NUT FREE

PREP TIME: 10 MINUTES • COOK TIME: 25 MINUTES • SERVES 4

This recipe was my mother's choice whenever she wanted a quick dinner option. She called it *beed be banadora*—eggs in tomatoes. Fresh tomatoes make a huge difference in this dish, but a 15-ounce can of diced tomatoes will work in a pinch. It also makes a great addition to your brunch recipe arsenal. Serve crispy toast or pita bread alongside it for dipping—and to get every bit of the delicious spicy tomato sauce.

¼ cup olive oil

1 onion, finely chopped

1 cup chopped green bell pepper

2 garlic cloves, minced

3 ripe tomatoes, diced

1 teaspoon paprika

½ teaspoon ground cumin

½ teaspoon red pepper flakes

⅛ teaspoon salt

4 medium eggs

1. In a large sauté pan or skillet over medium heat, heat the olive oil.
2. Add the onion and green bell pepper. Cook for about 8 minutes until the vegetables soften. Add the garlic and cook for 1 minute more.
3. In a small bowl, stir together the tomatoes, paprika, cumin, red pepper flakes, and salt until well combined. Add the tomato mixture to the pan, stir, and simmer for 8 minutes.
4. Gently crack the eggs on top of the cooked vegetables, being careful not to break the yolks. Cover the pan and cook for 5 minutes or until the egg yolks are firm but not dry.

PER SERVING: CALORIES: 225; TOTAL FAT: 19G; SATURATED FAT: 3G; CARBOHYDRATES: 10G; FIBER: 2G; PROTEIN: 7G; SODIUM: 143MG

ASPARAGUS AND SWISS QUICHE

NUT FREE

PREP TIME: 20 MINUTES • COOK TIME: 50 MINUTES • SERVES 6

While I was growing up, my mom never used asparagus in any of her cooking, so I never had it until I came to America. A family in Washington, DC, hosted some foreign students for dinner, which included many dishes—and one was seared fresh asparagus. I had no idea what it was. I watched the hostess eat it, and I copied her. To my surprise, I loved it. Here it brings freshness to the perfect springtime meal.

6 cups water

8 ounces asparagus, ends trimmed, cut into 1-inch pieces

2 tablespoons olive oil

4 scallions, white and green parts, chopped

1 (8-inch) store-bought unbaked pie shell

2 large eggs

½ cup heavy cream

2 tablespoons chopped fresh tarragon

¼ teaspoon ground nutmeg

1 cup shredded Swiss cheese

1. Preheat the oven to 400°F.
2. In a medium pot over medium-high heat, bring the water to a boil. Drop the asparagus into the boiling water and blanch for 2 minutes. Drain and set aside.
3. In a skillet over medium heat, heat the olive oil. Add the scallions and cook for 5 minutes. Add the asparagus and cook for 1 minute.
4. Spoon the vegetables into the unbaked pie shell. Set aside.
5. In a medium bowl, whisk the eggs. Add the heavy cream, tarragon, and nutmeg. Whisk to combine well.
6. Pour the egg mixture over the asparagus. Sprinkle the Swiss cheese over the top.
7. Bake for about 40 minutes until firm. Remove from the oven, cool to room temperature, and serve.

PER SERVING: CALORIES: 319; TOTAL FAT: 26G; SATURATED FAT: 10G; CARBOHYDRATES: 15G; FIBER: 1G; PROTEIN: 9G; SODIUM: 202MG

HERBS, CHEESE, AND PINE NUT FRITTATA

GLUTEN FREE

PREP TIME: 20 MINUTES • COOK TIME: 30 MINUTES • SERVES 4

I love texture—I always say our teeth are here for a reason—which is why I add nuts or seeds to most of my dishes. Here I add pine nuts to a delicious herb and cheese–filled frittata to give it some bite. This dish is great for breakfast, lunch, or dinner, and leftovers can be kept wrapped in the refrigerator for up to five days.

¼ cup olive oil

2 tablespoons chopped scallion, white part only

1 garlic clove, coarsely chopped

1 (16-ounce) package frozen chopped spinach, thawed

¼ cup pine nuts

2 tablespoons chopped fresh chives

1 tablespoon chopped fresh basil

1 tablespoon chopped fresh thyme

1 teaspoon dried oregano

3 large eggs

3 tablespoons heavy cream

½ cup grated Gruyère cheese

1. In a large skillet over medium heat, heat the olive oil. Add the scallion and garlic and cook for 5 minutes.
2. Add the spinach, pine nuts, chives, basil, thyme, and oregano. Cook, stirring, for 5 minutes. Remove from the heat and drain any liquid. Set aside.
3. In a small bowl, whisk the eggs, heavy cream, and Gruyère cheese. Pour the egg mixture into the spinach mixture and stir well.
4. Return the skillet to medium heat and cook the frittata for about 15 minutes or until set. Press the top with a spatula to compact the ingredients.
5. Remove from the heat, cover the skillet with a large plate, and carefully flip the frittata onto the plate. Slide the frittata back into the skillet and cook over medium heat for about 5 minutes until golden.

PER SERVING: CALORIES: 346; TOTAL FAT: 31G; SATURATED FAT: 9G; CARBOHYDRATES: 7G; FIBER: 3G; PROTEIN: 14G; SODIUM: 193MG

SUBSTITUTION TIP: Some people have pine nut syndrome. If they eat more than 1 teaspoon of pine nuts in one meal, the other foods they consume will taste bitter and metallic. Fortunately, this lasts only a few days. You can use slivered almonds instead of pine nuts, just in case.

ZUCCHINI, ONION, AND PARMESAN FRITTATA

GLUTEN FREE ✦ NUT FREE

PREP TIME: 15 MINUTES • COOK TIME: 30 MINUTES • SERVES 6

The word *frittata* is Italian for "fried." Similar to a crustless quiche, there are so many varieties that you can make a different frittata each day of the month without repeating. Use feta cheese, chopped bell pepper, and oregano for a Greek influence. Or try kale, goat cheese, and thyme for a French flair. This recipe, a personal favorite, leans heavily on Italian flavors.

¼ cup olive oil

1 red onion, chopped

2 zucchini, diced

6 large eggs

¼ cup milk

¼ cup chopped fresh parsley

¼ cup freshly grated Parmesan cheese

1 teaspoon dried basil

⅛ teaspoon salt

⅛ teaspoon freshly ground black pepper

1. Preheat the oven to 350°F.
2. In a 12-inch ovenproof skillet over medium heat, heat the olive oil.
3. Add the red onion and cook for 2 minutes. Add the zucchini and sauté for 10 minutes. Remove from the heat.
4. In a medium bowl, whisk the eggs, milk, parsley, Parmesan cheese, basil, salt, and pepper until combined. Pour the egg mixture over the vegetables.
5. Place the skillet in the oven and bake for 15 minutes or until the center of the frittata is set. Serve hot.

PER SERVING: CALORIES: 182; TOTAL FAT: 15G; SATURATED FAT: 4G; CARBOHYDRATES: 5G; FIBER: 1G; PROTEIN: 8G; SODIUM: 169MG

SPINACH AND MUSHROOM GRATIN

GLUTEN FREE ✦ NUT FREE

PREP TIME: 10 MINUTES • COOK TIME: 40 MINUTES • SERVES 8

I used to fear mushrooms. When I was about 10, I learned in science class that 20 percent of mushrooms can make you sick and 1 percent can kill you—so I stopped eating them. In high school, when I noticed my family was still healthy after eating mushrooms, I gave them another chance, and I'm glad I did because I would never have tasted this wonderfully creamy, umami-filled dish! I use shiitake mushrooms, but use any kind of mushroom you have on hand.

4 tablespoons butter

1 large onion, chopped

1 pound shiitake mushrooms, coarsely chopped

1 cup heavy cream

1 cup milk

2 tablespoons cornstarch

2 tablespoons cold water

¼ teaspoon grated nutmeg

⅛ teaspoon salt

⅛ teaspoon freshly ground black pepper

1 (16-ounce) package frozen chopped spinach, thawed and squeezed dry

½ cup freshly grated Parmesan cheese

½ cup grated Gruyère cheese

1. Preheat the oven to 400°F.
2. In a heavy-bottomed saucepan over medium heat, melt the butter. Add the onion and cook for 5 minutes. Add the mushrooms and cook for 10 minutes or until browned.
3. In a small bowl, whisk the heavy cream and milk.
4. In another small bowl, stir together the cornstarch and cold water until the cornstarch dissolves. Add this slurry to the milk mixture and stir to combine.
5. Pour the milk mixture over the mushrooms. Stir in the nutmeg, salt, and pepper. Cook for about 5 minutes until the sauce thickens.
6. Add the spinach to the sauce. Stir in the Parmesan cheese. Spoon the spinach and mushroom mixture into a gratin baking dish. Sprinkle the Gruyère cheese on top.
7. Bake for about 20 minutes until hot and bubbly.

PER SERVING: CALORIES: 278; TOTAL FAT: 22G; SATURATED FAT: 13G; CARBOHYDRATES: 16G; FIBER: 3G; PROTEIN: 9G; SODIUM: 368MG

CHERRY TOMATO, OLIVE, AND SOURDOUGH GRATIN

NUT FREE

PREP TIME: 20 MINUTES • COOK TIME: 45 MINUTES • SERVES 6

Mediterranean people love their fresh-baked bread and loathe wasting any of it, which is why so many recipes make use of bread that is slightly stale. Here, cubes of tangy sourdough are baked to crispy perfection and provide a great crunch to this Spanish-influenced gratin.

1 sourdough loaf, cut into 1-inch cubes (about 6 cups)

1 cup pitted cured black olives, halved lengthwise, divided

1 (12-ounce) can diced tomatoes

6 scallions, white and green parts, chopped

1 cup chopped fresh basil

⅛ teaspoon salt, plus more as needed

⅛ teaspoon freshly ground black pepper, plus more as needed

1 cup shredded Manchego cheese

4 cups cherry tomatoes, halved lengthwise

1. Preheat the oven to 375°F.
2. Place the bread in a large bowl. Chop half the olives and add them to the bread, along with the diced tomatoes, scallions, basil, salt, and pepper. Stir until well combined. Taste and season with more salt and pepper, as needed.
3. Spoon the mixture into a 9-by-13-inch baking dish. Top the bread mixture with the Manchego cheese. Arrange the cherry tomatoes and the remaining olives on top of the cheese. Cover the dish with aluminum foil.
4. Bake for 20 minutes. Remove the foil and bake for 15 minutes more until the cheese is melted and the edges of the bread are golden. Let rest for 10 minutes before serving.

PER SERVING: CALORIES: 324; TOTAL FAT: 11G; SATURATED FAT: 4G; CARBOHYDRATES: 42G; FIBER: 3G; PROTEIN: 13G; SODIUM: 536MG

SUBSTITUTION TIP: Replace the cured black olives with pitted Kalamata olives.

RATATOUILLE

GLUTEN FREE ✦ NUT FREE ✦ VEGAN

PREP TIME: 20 MINUTES • COOK TIME: 35 MINUTES • SERVES 4

Ratatouille is the French version of moussaka. Both dishes make wonderful use of Mediterranean summer vegetables. Each year when our local farm delivers the vegetables, I immediately start chopping everything to make my ratatouille. It's endlessly customizable. I've made ratatouille with butternut squash, green tomatoes, tarragon—you cannot go wrong with fresh vegetables and good olive oil.

¼ cup olive oil

1 onion, chopped

4 garlic cloves, crushed

1 large eggplant, cut into 1-inch cubes

1 zucchini, cut into 1-inch cubes

1 red bell pepper, seeded and chopped

⅛ teaspoon salt, plus more as needed

3 tomatoes, chopped

1 tablespoon dried oregano

1 teaspoon dried thyme

¼ cup chopped fresh basil

1. In a heavy-bottomed skillet over medium heat, heat the olive oil.
2. Add the onion and cook for 5 minutes or until soft. Add the garlic and cook for 2 minutes.
3. Add the eggplant and cook for 10 minutes, stirring often.
4. Stir in the zucchini, red bell pepper, and salt. Cook for 5 minutes.
5. Stir in the tomatoes, oregano, thyme, and basil. Cook for 10 minutes. Taste and season with more salt, as needed.

PER SERVING: CALORIES: 191; TOTAL FAT: 13G; SATURATED FAT: 2G; CARBOHYDRATES: 19G; FIBER: 7G; PROTEIN: 4G; SODIUM: 88MG

FRENCH BEAN STEW

GLUTEN FREE ✦ NUT FREE ✦ VEGAN

PREP TIME: 10 MINUTES • COOK TIME: 40 MINUTES • SERVES 4

Almost every country on the Mediterranean coast cooks different versions of this stew. In Syria and Turkey, this dish is flavored with cilantro; in Italy the stew is flavored with fresh basil; and in Morocco coriander and cumin are used. I stick to the classic French rendition, but I highly recommend trying the others to find your favorite.

¼ cup olive oil

1 onion, chopped

1 pound French green beans, trimmed and cut into 2-inch pieces

4 ripe tomatoes, seeded and diced, or 1 (28-ounce) can diced tomatoes, undrained

4 garlic cloves, minced

⅛ teaspoon salt

⅛ teaspoon freshly ground black pepper

2 tablespoons tomato paste

2 cups vegetable broth

1. In a soup pot over medium heat, heat the olive oil. Add the onion and cook for 5 minutes, stirring often, until softened.
2. Add the green beans, cover the pot, and cook for 10 minutes, stirring often. If necessary, add 2 tablespoons of water to prevent the beans from sticking.
3. Stir in the tomatoes and their juices, garlic, salt, and pepper. Cook for 10 minutes.
4. In a medium bowl, whisk the tomato paste and vegetable broth until completely combined. Pour the broth into the pot. Bring the stew to a boil. Cover the pot and simmer for 15 minutes.
5. Taste and season with more salt and pepper, as needed, before serving.

PER SERVING: CALORIES: 207; TOTAL FAT: 14G; SATURATED FAT: 2G; CARBOHYDRATES: 18G; FIBER: 6G; PROTEIN: 6G; SODIUM: 378MG

PREP TIP: You can use frozen cut French green beans to save time. There is no need to thaw them first.

EGGPLANT AND LENTIL TAGINE

GLUTEN FREE ✦ NUT FREE ✦ VEGAN

PREP TIME: 15 MINUTES • COOK TIME: 40 MINUTES • SERVES 6

When I opened my restaurant in South Dakota 15 years ago, I would use 10 pounds of eggplant making moussaka. These days I use about 100 pounds a week to make many eggplant dishes, including this delicious stew. People always tell me, "This is one of your best lentil dishes!" Or "I never thought my husband would eat eggplant—but he loves this dish." On the rare occasion we have leftovers, especially in winter, I like to add extra water and a couple tablespoons more of tomato paste to create a hearty soup.

1 eggplant, cut into 1-inch cubes

½ cup olive oil, divided

2 onions, thinly sliced

1 cup chopped fresh cilantro

3 tablespoons tomato paste

2 tablespoons Harissa (page 143), or store-bought

2 teaspoons ground coriander

1 teaspoon ground cumin

1 pound dried brown lentils, rinsed and picked over for debris

8 cups water

⅛ teaspoon salt, plus more as needed

1. Preheat the broiler.
2. In a medium bowl, toss the eggplant with 2 tablespoons of olive oil to coat. Transfer to a baking sheet and broil for about 5 minutes until golden. Remove and set aside.
3. In a large soup pot over medium heat, heat the remaining 6 tablespoons of olive oil.
4. Add the onions and cook for about 8 minutes until golden. Add the cilantro and cook for 1 minute. Using a slotted spoon, transfer half the onion mixture to a bowl and set aside.
5. Add the tomato paste, harissa, coriander, and cumin to the pot. Stir to combine and cook for 1 minute.
6. Stir in the lentils, water, salt, and pepper. Taste and season with more salt and pepper, as needed. Increase the heat to bring the mixture to a boil. Reduce the heat to medium and cook for about 15 minutes or until the lentils are tender.

⅛ teaspoon freshly ground black pepper, plus more as needed

2 cups fresh baby spinach

1 cup diced dried apricots

½ cup freshly squeezed lemon juice

2 tablespoons chopped Preserved Lemons (page 147), or store-bought

7. Stir in the eggplant, spinach, apricots, lemon juice, and preserved lemons. Cook for 10 minutes more.

8. Spoon the tagine onto a platter and top with the remaining cooked onion and cilantro mixture.

PER SERVING: CALORIES: 526; TOTAL FAT: 18G; SATURATED FAT: 3G; CARBOHYDRATES: 72G; FIBER: 29G; PROTEIN: 23G; SODIUM: 82MG

PREP TIP: I don't peel the eggplant. The skin is high in nutrients and adds fiber and texture.

ROASTED CAULIFLOWER TAGINE

GLUTEN FREE ✦ NUT FREE ✦ VEGAN

PREP TIME: 15 MINUTES • COOK TIME: 35 MINUTES • SERVES 6

Any dish with mixed vegetables, sauce, and a protein is called *tagine* in North Africa, *yakhneh* in the Eastern Mediterranean, and *stew* in the United States. This version, featuring cauliflower, potatoes, tomatoes, and chickpeas, tastes great over rice or couscous.

2 cauliflower heads, cut into florets

½ cup olive oil, divided

½ cup chopped fresh cilantro

1 onion, chopped

6 garlic cloves, peeled

1 teaspoon ground coriander

1 (32-ounce) can diced tomatoes

1 tablespoon tomato paste

6 cups water

⅛ teaspoon salt, plus more as needed

⅛ teaspoon freshly ground black pepper, plus more as needed

2 large russet potatoes, peeled and cut into 1-inch cubes

1 (15-ounce) can chickpeas, drained and rinsed

¼ cup chopped Preserved Lemons (page 147), or store-bought

1. Preheat the broiler.
2. In a medium bowl, toss the cauliflower and 2 tablespoons of olive oil until well coated. Transfer the florets to a baking sheet and broil for about 5 minutes until golden. Remove and set aside.
3. In a small skillet over medium heat, heat 2 tablespoons of olive oil. Add the cilantro and sear for a few seconds. Set aside.
4. In a heavy-bottomed pot over medium heat, heat the remaining 4 tablespoons of olive oil. Add the onion and sauté for 2 to 3 minutes until golden. Stir in the garlic and coriander. Cook for 1 minute more.
5. Stir in the tomatoes, tomato paste, water, salt, and pepper until well combined. Taste and season with more salt and pepper, as needed. Increase the heat to medium-high and bring to a boil. Turn the heat to low and simmer for 5 minutes.
6. Stir in the potatoes, increase the heat to high, and return the mixture to a boil. Reduce the heat to medium and cook for about 10 minutes until the potatoes are fork-tender but not overcooked.
7. Add the chickpeas, roasted cauliflower, and cilantro. Stir gently and cook over low heat for 10 minutes to warm through. Sprinkle with the preserved lemons and serve.

PER SERVING: CALORIES: 378; TOTAL FAT: 19G; SATURATED FAT: 3G; CARBOHYDRATES: 48G; FIBER: 13G; PROTEIN: 11G; SODIUM: 126MG

EGGPLANT MOUSSAKA

FREEZER FRIENDLY ✦ GLUTEN FREE ✦ NUT FREE

PREP TIME: 30 MINUTES • COOK TIME: 1 HOUR, 30 MINUTES • SERVES 6

Although preparing these components separately might seem daunting, it's worth the time and effort! You can use store-bought sauce to reduce prep, and it's the perfect recipe to use up leftover Basic Tomato Basil Sauce (page 145) and Béchamel Sauce (page 146), if you have it. This dish can also be made a couple days ahead of time. Refrigerate covered, and when ready to serve, increase the baking time by 10 minutes.

FOR THE EGGPLANT

4 eggplants, cut into
½-inch-thick rounds

Olive oil, for brushing

FOR THE TOMATO SAUCE

½ cup olive oil

2 large onions, thinly sliced

2 large red bell peppers,
seeded and cut into
½-inch-thick slices

1 (28-ounce) can
diced tomatoes

2 tablespoons tomato paste

1 teaspoon dried oregano

⅛ teaspoon salt

TO MAKE THE EGGPLANT

1. Preheat the broiler.
2. Place the eggplant slices on a baking sheet. Brush lightly with olive oil. Broil for about 5 minutes until golden. Remove and set aside.

TO MAKE THE TOMATO SAUCE

1. In a medium saucepan over medium heat, heat the olive oil.
2. Add the onions and cook for about 8 minutes, stirring often, until golden.
3. Add the red bell peppers and cook for 2 minutes.
4. Stir in the tomatoes, tomato paste, oregano, and salt. Increase the heat and bring the sauce to a boil. Reduce the heat to medium, cover the pan, and simmer for 10 minutes.

FOR THE CHEESE SAUCE

4 cups milk

¼ cup cornstarch

½ cup water

1 cup crumbled feta cheese

1 teaspoon dried oregano

TO MAKE THE CHEESE SAUCE

1. In a medium saucepan over medium heat, heat the milk for about 5 minutes until it starts to warm. Set aside.
2. In a small bowl, whisk the cornstarch and water until the cornstarch dissolves. Add this slurry to the heated milk. Place the pan over medium heat and cook for about 15 minutes, stirring continuously, until the sauce thickens. Remove from the heat and stir in the feta cheese and oregano.

TO ASSEMBLE

1. Preheat the oven to 375°F.
2. In a 9-by-13-inch baking dish, arrange half the eggplant slices in a single layer.
3. Spoon half the tomato sauce evenly over the eggplant. Repeat with the remaining eggplant and tomato sauce.
4. Spread the cheese sauce over the top.
5. Bake for about 40 minutes until golden.

PER SERVING: CALORIES: 465; TOTAL FAT: 27G; SATURATED FAT: 8G; CARBOHYDRATES: 50G; FIBER: 17G; PROTEIN: 15G; SODIUM: 429MG

EGGPLANT PARMESAN

NUT FREE

PREP TIME: 30 MINUTES • COOK TIME: 1 HOUR, 20 MINUTES • SERVES 6

During summer, I broil slices of eggplant, place them in freezer bags, and freeze to make eggplant dishes throughout the year. This is one of my favorite dishes. When shopping for eggplants, look for small or medium ones. They tend to have fewer seeds, which means they will be less bitter. Make sure the eggplant feels firm to the touch and is heavy for its size. The skin should be shiny and the stem should be green—all signs that the eggplant has been recently harvested.

2 cups bread crumbs

1 teaspoon dried oregano

¼ teaspoon salt

1 cup skim milk

12 small or 6 medium eggplants, cut into ½-inch-thick slices

3 cups Basic Tomato Basil Sauce (page 145), or store-bought

4 cups diced fresh mozzarella cheese

1 cup freshly grated Parmesan cheese

1. Preheat the oven to 375°F.
2. In a large bowl, stir together the bread crumbs, oregano, and salt. Pour the milk into another large bowl.
3. Dip the eggplant slices in the milk and then in the bread crumb mixture. Place the coated eggplant slices on a baking sheet.
4. Bake for 30 minutes. Remove and set aside.
5. Spread a few spoonfuls of the tomato sauce on the bottom of a 9-by-13-inch baking dish. Arrange half the eggplant over the sauce. Cover the eggplant with the mozzarella cheese. Top with the remaining eggplant. Spoon the remaining tomato sauce over the eggplant. Cover the sauce with the Parmesan cheese.
6. Bake for 40 minutes. Let rest for 10 minutes before serving.

PER SERVING: CALORIES: 490; TOTAL FAT: 22G; SATURATED FAT: 13G; CARBOHYDRATES: 46G; FIBER: 14G; PROTEIN: 31G; SODIUM: 654MG

SUBSTITUTION TIP: Using gluten-free bread crumbs is an easy way to make this a gluten-free dish.

MUSHROOM PASTILLA

PREP TIME: 30 MINUTES • COOK TIME: 35 MINUTES • SERVES 4

Pastilla is a Moroccan meat pie, sometimes called "pigeon pie" because, traditionally, it was made by stuffing flaky filo dough with spiced pigeon meat, apricots, and eggs. I've traded the pigeon for mushrooms and a delicious blend of spices. I like to use cremini mushrooms, but use any kind you have on hand. The powdered sugar sprinkled at the end might seem unexpected, but its sweetness complements the flavors in this dish.

3 large eggs

¼ cup olive oil

1 onion, chopped

1 pound mushrooms, chopped

1 teaspoon ground cinnamon, divided

½ teaspoon ground allspice

½ teaspoon ground ginger

½ teaspoon ground coriander

½ cup chopped fresh parsley

1 tablespoon freshly squeezed lemon juice

½ cup toasted slivered almonds

Salt

Freshly ground black pepper

8 sheets filo dough; follow the instructions on the package to prevent drying

4 tablespoons butter, melted

1 tablespoon powdered sugar

1. Preheat the oven to 400°F.
2. In a small bowl, whisk the eggs and set aside.
3. In a skillet over medium heat, heat the olive oil.
4. Add the onion and sauté for 5 minutes or until softened. Add the mushrooms and cook for 5 minutes. Stir in ½ teaspoon of cinnamon, the allspice, ginger, coriander, parsley, and lemon juice.
5. Add the eggs to the skillet. Cook for about 3 minutes, stirring, until the eggs are fully cooked.
6. Add the almonds. Season the mixture with salt and pepper and set aside.
7. One at a time, brush both sides of each filo sheet with melted butter and layer into an 8-inch round baking dish.
8. Spoon the mushroom filling in the center of the dough and spread it evenly. Fold the extra dough over the filling, making sure all the filling is covered. Brush the top with the remaining melted butter.
9. Bake for 15 to 20 minutes or until the filo is golden brown.
10. Dust with the powdered sugar and remaining ½ teaspoon of cinnamon. Serve hot.

PER SERVING: CALORIES: 507; TOTAL FAT: 38G; SATURATED FAT: 12G; CARBOHYDRATES: 33G; FIBER: 5G; PROTEIN: 14G; SODIUM: 270MG

VARIATION TIP: Add chopped apricots and raisins for sweeter flavors.

RICE, GRAINS, AND BEANS

RICE WITH VERMICELLI

NUT FREE ✦ VEGAN

PREP TIME: 5 MINUTES • COOK TIME: 45 MINUTES • SERVES 6

Rice with vermicelli is a popular side dish in the Mediterranean area. My daughter had it for the first time when we visited my family in Syria. After that, whenever she wanted me to make the dish, she would ask for *sito* ("grandmother") rice with spaghetti. This rice goes great with Roasted Cauliflower Tagine (page 84), Eggplant Moussaka (page 86), or topped with Roasted Root Vegetables (page 56).

2 cups short-grain rice

3½ cups water, plus more for rinsing and soaking the rice

¼ cup olive oil

1 cup broken vermicelli pasta

Salt

1. Rinse the rice under cold water until the water runs clean. Place the rice in a bowl, cover with water, and let soak for 10 minutes. Drain and set aside.
2. In a medium pot over medium heat, heat the olive oil.
3. Stir in the vermicelli and cook for 2 to 3 minutes, stirring continuously, until golden. (Watch it! It happens fast.)
4. Add the rice and cook for 1 minute, stirring, so the rice is well coated in the oil.
5. Add the water and a pinch of salt and bring the liquid to a boil. Reduce the heat to low, cover the pot, and simmer for 20 minutes.
6. Remove from the heat and let rest, covered, for 10 minutes. Fluff with a fork and serve.

PER SERVING: CALORIES: 346; TOTAL FAT: 9G; SATURATED FAT: 1G; CARBOHYDRATES: 60G; FIBER: 2G; PROTEIN: 7G; SODIUM: 28MG

FAVA BEANS AND RICE

GLUTEN FREE ✦ VEGAN

PREP TIME: 10 MINUTES • COOK TIME: 35 MINUTES • SERVES 4

Fava beans, also known as broad beans, are a popular ingredient around the Mediterranean despite the fact that they have a very short harvest season. Fava-based dishes, like this simple one-pot side dish, reach their peak in April and May, so be on the lookout to make sure you find them at the height of freshness.

¼ cup olive oil

4 cups fresh fava beans, shelled

4½ cups water, plus more for drizzling

2 cups basmati rice

⅛ teaspoon salt

⅛ teaspoon freshly ground black pepper

2 tablespoons pine nuts, toasted

½ cup chopped fresh garlic chives, or fresh onion chives

1. In a large saucepan over medium heat, heat the olive oil.
2. Add the fava beans and drizzle them with a bit of water to avoid burning or sticking. Cook for 10 minutes.
3. Gently stir in the rice. Add the water, salt, and pepper. Increase the heat and bring the mixture to a boil. Cover the pan, reduce the heat to low, and simmer for 15 minutes.
4. Turn off the heat and let the mixture rest for 10 minutes before serving. Spoon onto a serving platter and sprinkle with the toasted pine nuts and chives.

PER SERVING: CALORIES: 587; TOTAL FAT: 17G; SATURATED FAT: 2G; CARBOHYDRATES: 97G; FIBER: 2G; PROTEIN: 17G; SODIUM: 110MG

SUBSTITUTION TIP: Use lima beans if you cannot find fava beans.

BUTTERED FAVA BEANS

GLUTEN FREE ✦ NUT FREE

PREP TIME: 30 MINUTES • COOK TIME: 15 MINUTES • SERVES 4

If you can't tell I love fava beans by the number of recipes in this book, know that I once asked a local farmer to plant some for me. He'd never heard of fava beans and was not sure they would sell in South Dakota. I promised to buy any fava beans he could grow—and I did. I posted photos of the fresh fava beans on my restaurant's Facebook page and received so many messages asking for the source. I showed that to the farmer—and he promised to plant more next year. (And, I confess, I did not share my fava beans with anyone!)

½ cup vegetable broth

4 pounds fava beans, shelled

¼ cup fresh tarragon, divided

1 teaspoon chopped
   fresh thyme

¼ teaspoon freshly ground
   black pepper

⅛ teaspoon salt

2 tablespoons butter

1 garlic clove, minced

2 tablespoons chopped
   fresh parsley

1. In a shallow pan over medium heat, bring the vegetable broth to a boil.
2. Add the fava beans, 2 tablespoons of tarragon, the thyme, pepper, and salt. Cook for about 10 minutes until the broth is almost absorbed and the beans are tender.
3. Stir in the butter, garlic, and remaining 2 tablespoons of tarragon. Cook for 2 to 3 minutes.
4. Sprinkle with the parsley and serve hot.

PER SERVING: CALORIES: 458; TOTAL FAT: 9G; SATURATED FAT: 4G; CARBOHYDRATES: 81G; FIBER: 0G; PROTEIN: 37G; SODIUM: 230MG

VARIATION TIP: If you cannot find fresh fava beans, use frozen, shelled lima beans instead. Just thaw and follow the recipe as written.

FREEKEH

PREP TIME: 10 MINUTES • COOK TIME: 40 MINUTES • SERVES 4

Freekeh is durum wheat harvested while still green and then roasted. This method of harvesting, roasting, and processing gives the finished wheat smoky, nutty flavors. Recently, I decided to introduce my customers to freekeh during a dinner buffet. It was a tremendous success. If, by any chance, you have leftovers of this delicious dish, toss in some chopped cucumber, tomato, and parsley and you will have a delicious and healthy salad.

4 tablespoons Ghee
  (page 148), or store-bought

1 onion, chopped

3½ cups vegetable broth

1 teaspoon ground allspice

2 cups freekeh

2 tablespoons pine
  nuts, toasted

1. In a heavy-bottomed saucepan over medium heat, melt the ghee.
2. Stir in the onion and cook for about 5 minutes, stirring constantly, until the onion is golden.
3. Pour in the vegetable broth, add the allspice, and bring to a boil.
4. Stir in the freekeh and return the mixture to a boil. Reduce the heat to low, cover the pan, and simmer for 30 minutes, stirring occasionally.
5. Spoon the freekeh into a serving dish and top with the toasted pine nuts.

PER SERVING: CALORIES: 459; TOTAL FAT: 18G; SATURATED FAT: 8G; CARBOHYDRATES: 64G; FIBER: 10G; PROTEIN: 19G; SODIUM: 124MG

FRIED RICE BALLS WITH TOMATO SAUCE

GLUTEN FREE ✦ NUT FREE

PREP TIME: 15 MINUTES • COOK TIME: 20 MINUTES • MAKES 8 BALLS

Traditionally called *arancini*, these stuffed fried rice balls are a family favorite. It's hard to wait for these bites to cool a bit before digging in, but the roof of your mouth will thank you. Stuff them with cooked chopped vegetables for a healthier option.

1 cup bread crumbs

2 cups cooked risotto (see tip)

2 large eggs, divided

¼ cup freshly grated Parmesan cheese

8 fresh baby mozzarella balls, or 1 (4-inch) log fresh mozzarella, cut into 8 pieces

2 tablespoons water

1 cup corn oil

1 cup Basic Tomato Basil Sauce (page 145), or store-bought

INGREDIENT TIP: You can prepare the Asparagus Risotto (page 102) for this recipe. Follow the instructions as written but don't add the asparagus.

1. Pour the bread crumbs into a small bowl and set aside.
2. In a medium bowl, stir together the risotto, 1 egg, and the Parmesan cheese until well combined.
3. Moisten your hands with a little water to prevent sticking and divide the risotto mixture into 8 pieces. Place them on a clean work surface and flatten each piece.
4. Place 1 mozzarella ball on each flattened rice disk. Close the rice around the mozzarella to form a ball. Repeat until you finish all the balls.
5. In the same medium, now-empty bowl, whisk the remaining egg and the water.
6. Dip each prepared risotto ball into the egg wash and roll it in the bread crumbs. Set aside.
7. In a large sauté pan or skillet over high heat, heat the corn oil for about 3 minutes.
8. Gently lower the risotto balls into the hot oil and fry for 5 to 8 minutes until golden brown. Stir them, as needed, to ensure the entire surface is fried. Using a slotted spoon, transfer the fried balls to paper towels to drain.
9. In a medium saucepan over medium heat, heat the tomato sauce for 5 minutes, stirring occasionally, and serve the warm sauce alongside the rice balls.

PER SERVING: CALORIES: 255; TOTAL FAT: 15G; SATURATED FAT: 6G; CARBOHYDRATES: 16G; FIBER: 2G; PROTEIN: 11G; SODIUM: 290MG

SPANISH-STYLE RICE

GLUTEN FREE ✦ NUT FREE ✦ VEGAN

PREP TIME: 10 MINUTES • COOK TIME: 35 MINUTES • SERVES 4

Rice dishes in Spain are usually yellow in color due to the addition of the popular local spice, saffron. However, saffron is expensive—it is considered the most expensive spice in the world!—and can be hard to come by. To make it more accessible, I've adapted one of the few red Spanish rice recipes. The beautiful color of this dish comes from tomato paste and paprika.

¼ cup olive oil

1 small onion, finely chopped

1 red bell pepper, seeded and diced

1½ cups white rice

1 teaspoon sweet paprika

½ teaspoon ground cumin

½ teaspoon ground coriander

1 garlic clove, minced

3 tablespoons tomato paste

3 cups vegetable broth

⅛ teaspoon salt, plus more as needed

1. In a large heavy-bottomed skillet over medium heat, heat the olive oil.
2. Stir in the onion and red bell pepper. Cook for 5 minutes or until softened.
3. Add the rice, paprika, cumin, and coriander and cook for 2 minutes, stirring often.
4. Add the garlic, tomato paste, vegetable broth, and salt. Stir to combine, taste, and season with more salt, as needed.
5. Increase the heat to bring the mixture to a boil. Reduce the heat to low, cover the skillet, and simmer for 20 minutes.
6. Let the rice rest, covered, for 5 minutes before serving.

PER SERVING: CALORIES: 414; TOTAL FAT: 14G; SATURATED FAT: 2G; CARBOHYDRATES: 63G; FIBER: 2G; PROTEIN: 6G; SODIUM: 196MG

ZUCCHINI WITH RICE AND TZATZIKI

GLUTEN FREE

PREP TIME: 20 MINUTES • COOK TIME: 35 MINUTES • SERVES 4

Zucchini is such a healthy vegetable: It contains antioxidants and anti-inflammatory phytonutrients and is an excellent source of B vitamins. Families around the Mediterranean region have figured out many ways to make this powerhouse delicious to take advantage of its many benefits. One of the most popular methods, as I'm sure you know, is to stuff it, but they also love to cook it with grains, as in this dish.

¼ cup olive oil

1 onion, chopped

3 zucchini, diced

1 cup vegetable broth

½ cup chopped fresh dill

Salt

Freshly ground black pepper

1 cup short-grain rice

2 tablespoons pine nuts, or slivered almonds, toasted (see tip)

1 cup Tzatziki Sauce (page 144), Plain Yogurt (page 150), or store-bought

1. In a heavy-bottomed pot over medium heat, heat the olive oil.
2. Add the onion, turn the heat to medium-low, and sauté for 5 minutes.
3. Add the zucchini and cook for 2 minutes more.
4. Stir in the vegetable broth and dill and season with salt and pepper. Increase the heat to medium and bring the mixture to a boil.
5. Stir in the rice and return the mixture to a boil. Reduce the heat to very low, cover the pot, and cook for 15 minutes. Remove from the heat and let the rice rest, covered, for 10 minutes.
6. Spoon the rice onto a serving platter, sprinkle with the pine nuts, and serve with tzatziki sauce.

PER SERVING: CALORIES: 414; TOTAL FAT: 17G; SATURATED FAT: 3G; CARBOHYDRATES: 57G; FIBER: 5G; PROTEIN: 11G; SODIUM: 286MG

INGREDIENT TIP: Toasting nuts enhances the flavor. To toast pine nuts, arrange them in an even layer on a baking sheet. Bake in a 350°F oven for 4 to 5 minutes or until the nuts are golden brown.

SLOW-COOKER BEANS

One of the easiest ways I've found to cook big batches of beans in advance is to use my slow cooker. You can buy dried beans in bulk and use my hands-off method, so anytime you need beans for stew, a pilaf, or a salad, all you have to do is to reach into your freezer! I have one shelf in my freezer filled with layers of bags of cooked chickpeas, cooked cannellini beans, cooked black beans, and cooked kidney beans.

In a slow cooker, combine 1 pound of dried beans with enough water to cover by at least 4 inches. Cover the cooker and cook on high heat for 3 to 5 hours. Check for doneness after 3 hours. Once fully cooked, drain and use immediately, or let cool and spoon into freezer bags to use later.

CANNELLINI BEANS WITH ROSEMARY AND GARLIC AIOLI

30 MINUTES OR LESS ✦ DAIRY FREE ✦ GLUTEN FREE ✦ NUT FREE

PREP TIME: 10 MINUTES • COOK TIME: 10 MINUTES • SERVES 4

Cannellini beans look like kidney beans, so sometimes people refer to them as white kidney beans or confuse them with great northern beans, but cannellini beans are meatier and have a nutty flavor. There is a restaurant in Rome that displays large glass jars filled with simmering cannellini beans for passersby to enjoy. This dish is wonderful on its own or served on crispy toast or as a dip for crackers.

4 cups cooked cannellini beans (see tip)

4 cups water

½ teaspoon salt

3 tablespoons olive oil

2 tablespoons chopped fresh rosemary

½ cup Garlic Aioli (page 142)

¼ teaspoon freshly ground black pepper

1. In a medium saucepan over medium heat, combine the cannellini beans, water, and salt. Bring to a boil. Cook for 5 minutes. Drain.
2. In a skillet over medium heat, heat the olive oil.
3. Add the beans. Stir in the rosemary and aioli. Reduce the heat to medium-low and cook, stirring, just to heat through. Season with pepper and serve.

PER SERVING: CALORIES: 545; TOTAL FAT: 36G; SATURATED FAT: 6G; CARBOHYDRATES: 42G; FIBER: 14G; PROTEIN: 15G; SODIUM: 448MG

INGREDIENT TIP: Use 3 (15.5-ounce) cans of cannellini beans for this recipe. There is no need to rinse or drain. You can also use great northern beans in place of cannellini beans.

JEWELED RICE

GLUTEN FREE ✦ VEGAN

PREP TIME: 15 MINUTES • COOK TIME: 30 MINUTES • SERVES 6

Full of vibrant colors, jeweled rice always takes center stage on the dining table. Its name comes from the gemstone colors provided by carrots, sweet peas, cranberries, and turmeric. This dish is usually served on special occasions, but it's so easy to make you can enjoy it anytime. Top it with chopped candied orange to give it a touch of sweetness.

½ cup olive oil, divided

1 onion, finely chopped

1 garlic clove, minced

½ teaspoon chopped peeled fresh ginger

4½ cups water

1 teaspoon salt, divided, plus more as needed

1 teaspoon ground turmeric

2 cups basmati rice

1 cup fresh sweet peas

2 carrots, peeled and cut into ½-inch dice

½ cup dried cranberries

Grated zest of 1 orange

⅛ teaspoon cayenne pepper

¼ cup slivered almonds, toasted

1. In a large heavy-bottomed pot over medium heat, heat ¼ cup of olive oil.
2. Add the onion and cook for 4 minutes. Add the garlic and ginger and cook for 1 minute more.
3. Stir in the water, ¾ teaspoon of salt, and the turmeric. Bring the mixture to a boil. Stir in the rice and return the mixture to a boil. Taste the broth and season with more salt, as needed. Reduce the heat to low, cover the pot, and cook for 15 minutes. Turn off the heat. Let the rice rest on the burner, covered, for 10 minutes.
4. Meanwhile, in a medium sauté pan or skillet over medium-low heat, heat the remaining ¼ cup of olive oil. Stir in the peas and carrots. Cook for 5 minutes.
5. Stir in the cranberries and orange zest. Season with the remaining ¼ teaspoon of salt and the cayenne. Cook for 1 to 2 minutes.
6. Spoon the rice onto a serving platter. Top with the peas and carrots and sprinkle with the toasted almonds.

PER SERVING: CALORIES: 460; TOTAL FAT: 19G; SATURATED FAT: 3G; CARBOHYDRATES: 65G; FIBER: 4G; PROTEIN: 7G; SODIUM: 307MG

SUBSTITUTION TIP: Use thawed frozen peas and frozen diced carrots instead of fresh. Cook for 2 minutes instead of 5.

ASPARAGUS RISOTTO

GLUTEN FREE ✦ NUT FREE

PREP TIME: 15 MINUTES • COOK TIME: 30 MINUTES • SERVES 4

Risotto is a classic rice dish of Northern Italy. You will find it as typical fare on restaurant menus in Milan, Venice, and Verona. In Italy, risotto, like pasta, is considered a first course—*primo piatto*—to be followed by the main dish. But any risotto dish can stand alone as a delicious main course.

5 cups vegetable broth, divided

3 tablespoons unsalted butter, divided

1 tablespoon olive oil

1 small onion, chopped

1½ cups Arborio rice

1 pound fresh asparagus, ends trimmed, cut into 1-inch pieces, tips separated

¼ cup freshly grated Parmesan cheese, plus more for serving

VARIATION TIP: Use other vegetables in place of asparagus. Try butternut squash, zucchini, or mushrooms. Sauté until cooked through and tender, and add to the risotto when you would add the asparagus tips.

1. In a saucepan over medium heat, bring the vegetable broth to a boil. Turn the heat to low and keep the broth at a steady simmer.
2. In a 4-quart heavy-bottomed saucepan over medium heat, melt 2 tablespoons of butter with the olive oil. Add the onion and cook for 2 to 3 minutes.
3. Add the rice and stir with a wooden spoon while cooking for 1 minute until the grains are well coated in the butter and oil.
4. Stir in ½ cup of warm broth. Cook, stirring often, for about 5 minutes until the broth is completely absorbed.
5. Add the asparagus stalks and another ½ cup of broth. Cook, stirring often, until the liquid is absorbed. Continue adding the broth, ½ cup at a time, and cooking until it is completely absorbed before adding the next ½ cup. Stir frequently to prevent sticking. After about 20 minutes, the rice should be cooked but still firm.
6. Add the asparagus tips, the remaining 1 tablespoon of butter, and the Parmesan cheese. Stir vigorously to combine.
7. Remove from the heat, top with additional Parmesan cheese, if desired, and serve immediately.

PER SERVING: CALORIES: 434; TOTAL FAT: 14G; SATURATED FAT: 7G; CARBOHYDRATES: 67G; FIBER: 6G; PROTEIN: 10G; SODIUM: 309MG

VEGETABLE PAELLA

GLUTEN FREE ✦ NUT FREE ✦ VEGAN

PREP TIME: 25 MINUTES • COOK TIME: 45 MINUTES • SERVES 6

Most experts agree that paella originated in Valencia, a port city on the southeastern coast of Spain, known as one of the region's biggest producers of rice. This beautiful dish actually gets its name from the pan it's cooked in—the flat, round paella pan—not from its ingredients. Don't worry if you don't have one; any large oven-safe skillet with deep sides will work.

¼ cup olive oil

1 large sweet onion, chopped

1 large red bell pepper, seeded and chopped

1 large green bell pepper, seeded and chopped

3 garlic cloves, finely minced

1 teaspoon smoked paprika

5 saffron threads (see tip)

1 zucchini, cut into ½-inch cubes

4 large ripe tomatoes, peeled, seeded, and chopped

1½ cups short-grain Spanish rice

3 cups vegetable broth, warmed

1. Preheat the oven to 350°F.
2. In a paella pan or large oven-safe skillet over medium heat, heat the olive oil.
3. Add the onion and red and green bell peppers and cook for 10 minutes.
4. Stir in the garlic, paprika, saffron threads, zucchini, and tomatoes. Turn the heat to medium-low and cook for 10 minutes.
5. Stir in the rice and vegetable broth. Increase the heat to bring the paella to a boil. Reduce the heat to medium-low and cook for 15 minutes. Cover the pan with aluminum foil and put it in the oven.
6. Bake for 10 minutes or until the broth is absorbed.

PER SERVING: CALORIES: 288; TOTAL FAT: 10G; SATURATED FAT: 1G; CARBOHYDRATES: 46G; FIBER: 3G; PROTEIN: 5G; SODIUM: 106MG

SUBSTITUTION TIP: Skip the saffron and use ¼ teaspoon ground turmeric instead to get the lovely yellow hue of traditional paella.

EGGPLANT AND RICE CASSEROLE

GLUTEN FREE ✦ VEGAN

PREP TIME: 30 MINUTES • COOK TIME: 35 MINUTES • SERVES 4

The original name of this meal translates to "Imam fainted." My favorite version of the origin is that an Imam was served this dish and loved it, but fainted when he found out how much it would cost him!

FOR THE SAUCE

½ cup olive oil

1 small onion, chopped

4 garlic cloves, mashed

6 ripe tomatoes, peeled and chopped

2 tablespoons tomato paste

1 teaspoon dried oregano

¼ teaspoon ground nutmeg

¼ teaspoon ground cumin

FOR THE CASSEROLE

4 (6-inch) Japanese eggplants, halved lengthwise

2 tablespoons olive oil

1 cup cooked rice

2 tablespoons pine nuts, toasted

1 cup water

TO MAKE THE SAUCE

1. In a heavy-bottomed saucepan over medium heat, heat the olive oil. Add the onion and cook for 5 minutes.
2. Stir in the garlic, tomatoes, tomato paste, oregano, nutmeg, and cumin. Bring to a boil. Cover, reduce heat to low, and simmer for 10 minutes. Remove and set aside.

TO MAKE THE CASSEROLE

1. Preheat the broiler.
2. While the sauce simmers, drizzle the eggplant with the olive oil and place them on a baking sheet. Broil for about 5 minutes until golden. Remove and let cool.
3. Turn the oven to 375°F. Arrange the cooled eggplant, cut-side up, in a 9-by-13-inch baking dish. Gently scoop out some flesh to make room for the stuffing.
4. In a bowl, combine half the tomato sauce, the cooked rice, and pine nuts. Fill each eggplant half with the rice mixture.
5. In the same bowl, combine the remaining tomato sauce and water. Pour over the eggplant.
6. Bake, covered, for 20 minutes until the eggplant is soft.

PER SERVING: CALORIES: 453; TOTAL FAT: 39G; SATURATED FAT: 5G; CARBOHYDRATES: 29G; FIBER: 7G; PROTEIN: 6G; SODIUM: 45MG

MANY VEGETABLE COUSCOUS

NUT FREE ✦ VEGAN

PREP TIME: 15 MINUTES • COOK TIME: 45 MINUTES • SERVES 8

In this recipe couscous serves as the base for a combination of perfectly spiced stewed vegetables, while whole jalapeños add a subtle kick to the broth.

¼ cup olive oil

1 onion, chopped

4 garlic cloves, minced

2 jalapeño peppers, pierced with a fork in several places

½ teaspoon ground cumin

½ teaspoon ground coriander

1 (28-ounce) can crushed tomatoes

2 tablespoons tomato paste

⅛ teaspoon salt

2 bay leaves

11 cups water, divided

4 carrots, peeled and cut into 2-inch pieces

2 zucchini, cut into 2-inch pieces

1 acorn squash, halved, seeded, and cut into 1-inch-thick slices

1 (15-ounce) can chickpeas, drained and rinsed

¼ cup chopped Preserved Lemons (page 147) (optional)

3 cups couscous

1. In a large heavy-bottomed pot over medium heat, heat the olive oil. Stir in the onion and cook for 4 minutes. Stir in the garlic, jalapeños, cumin, and coriander. Cook for 1 minute.
2. Add the tomatoes, tomato paste, salt, bay leaves, and 8 cups of water. Bring the mixture to a boil.
3. Add the carrots, zucchini, and acorn squash and return to a boil. Reduce the heat slightly, cover, and cook for about 20 minutes until the vegetables are tender but not mushy. Remove 2 cups of the cooking liquid and set aside. Season as needed.
4. Add the chickpeas and preserved lemons (if using). Cook for 2 to 3 minutes, and turn off the heat.
5. In a medium pan, bring the remaining 3 cups of water to a boil over high heat. Stir in the couscous, cover, and turn off the heat. Let the couscous rest for 10 minutes. Drizzle with 1 cup of reserved cooking liquid. Using a fork, fluff the couscous.
6. Mound it on a large platter. Drizzle it with the remaining cooking liquid. Remove the vegetables from the pot and arrange on top. Serve the remaining stew in a separate bowl.

PER SERVING: CALORIES: 415; TOTAL FAT: 7G; SATURATED FAT: 1G; CARBOHYDRATES: 75G; FIBER: 9G; PROTEIN: 14G; SODIUM: 306MG

KUSHARI

NUT FREE ✦ VEGAN

PREP TIME: 25 MINUTES • COOK TIME: 1 HOUR, 20 MINUTES • SERVES 8

This dish, rice mixed with beans, pasta, and hot sauce, is often called the national dish of Egypt and is a very popular street food. Making kushari is simple, but be warned that doing so requires the use of several pots, so it might be a little messy. In a kushari shop in Egypt, the server will spoon the rice into one container with each topping packed in a separate container so you can assemble it to your liking. To get this effect at home, spoon the rice and each topping into separate bowls, buffet style, and have each person assemble their own kushari.

FOR THE SAUCE

2 tablespoons olive oil

2 garlic cloves, minced

1 (16-ounce) can tomato sauce

¼ cup white vinegar

¼ cup Harissa (page 143), or store-bought

⅛ teaspoon salt

FOR THE RICE

1 cup olive oil

2 onions, thinly sliced

2 cups dried brown lentils, rinsed and picked over for debris

4 quarts plus ½ cup water, divided

2 cups short-grain rice

TO MAKE THE SAUCE

1. In a saucepan over medium heat, heat the olive oil.
2. Add the garlic and cook for 1 minute.
3. Stir in the tomato sauce, vinegar, harissa, and salt. Increase the heat to bring the sauce to a boil. Reduce the heat to low and cook for 20 minutes or until the sauce has thickened. Remove and set aside.

TO MAKE THE RICE

1. Line a plate with paper towels and set aside.
2. In a large pan over medium heat, heat the olive oil.
3. Add the onions and cook for 7 to 10 minutes, stirring often, until crisp and golden. Transfer the onions to the prepared plate and set aside. Reserve 2 tablespoons of the cooking oil. Reserve the pan.
4. In a large pot over high heat, combine the lentils and 4 cups of water. Bring to a boil and cook for 20 minutes. Drain, transfer to a bowl, and toss with the reserved 2 tablespoons of cooking oil. Set aside. Reserve the pot.

1 teaspoon salt, plus more for cooking the pasta

1 pound short elbow pasta

1 (15-ounce) can chickpeas, drained and rinsed

5. Place the pan you used to fry the onions over medium-high heat and add the rice, 4½ cups of water, and the salt to it. Bring to a boil. Reduce the heat to low, cover the pot, and cook for 20 minutes. Turn off the heat and let the rice rest for 10 minutes.

6. In the pot used to cook the lentils, bring the remaining 8 cups of water, salted, to a boil over high heat. Drop in the pasta and cook for 6 minutes or according to the package instructions. Drain and set aside.

TO ASSEMBLE

Spoon the rice onto a serving platter. Top it with the lentils, chickpeas, and pasta. Drizzle with the hot tomato sauce and sprinkle with the crispy fried onions.

PER SERVING: CALORIES: 668; TOTAL FAT: 13G; SATURATED FAT: 2G; CARBOHYDRATES: 113G; FIBER: 18G; PROTEIN: 25G; SODIUM: 321MG

BULGUR WITH TOMATOES AND CHICKPEAS

NUT FREE ✦ VEGAN

PREP TIME: 10 MINUTES • COOK TIME: 35 MINUTES • SERVES 6

This very simple meal is traditionally made by farmers in Eastern Mediterranean countries like Turkey and Syria. I love it because it's packed with great flavors and the bulgur provides fiber, protein, and iron. I make this dish once a month at my restaurant for my customers who won't stop asking for the "red bulgur dish." I like to serve it with sliced tomatoes and a simple, refreshing cucumber salad.

½ cup olive oil

1 onion, chopped

6 tomatoes, diced,
   or 1 (16-ounce) can
   diced tomatoes

2 tablespoons tomato paste

2 cups water

1 tablespoon Harissa
   (page 143), or store-bought

⅛ teaspoon salt

2 cups coarse bulgur #3

1 (15-ounce) can chickpeas,
   drained and rinsed

1. In a heavy-bottomed pot over medium heat, heat the olive oil.
2. Add the onion and sauté for 5 minutes.
3. Add the tomatoes with their juice and cook for 5 minutes.
4. Stir in the tomato paste, water, harissa, and salt. Bring to a boil.
5. Stir in the bulgur and chickpeas. Return the mixture to a boil. Reduce the heat to low, cover the pot, and cook for 15 minutes. Let rest for 15 minutes before serving.

PER SERVING: CALORIES: 413; TOTAL FAT: 19G; SATURATED FAT: 3G; CARBOHYDRATES: 55G; FIBER: 14G; PROTEIN: 11G; SODIUM: 103MG

SUBSTITUTION TIP: To make this dish gluten free, replace the bulgur with quinoa.

GREAT GRAINS, LEGUMES, AND COUSCOUS

Grains and legumes are crucial to Mediterranean cuisine, and as such, I use a variety in this book. Here's a bit more detail about them.

Brown lentils: These are the most common and least expensive variety of lentils. They cook in about 20 minutes and hold their shape well after cooking. They have an earthy flavor and I like to use these in soups.

Bulgur: Bulgur is cracked wheat that had been boiled, dried, and milled. Bulgur comes both coarsely and finely milled. Coarse bulgur, also called #3, is great for pilafs and soups. Fine bulgur requires no cooking, which makes it perfect for salads. Bulgur can be made with white wheat or red hard wheat. The color will be different but cooking times will be the same. I like to use the red bulgur in pilafs and white bulgur in salads.

Couscous: Couscous is actually a form of pasta, not a grain, made from semolina. Moroccan couscous is made by rubbing semolina between wet fingers until it forms tiny balls, which are then dried. It takes only 5 minutes to cook. Israeli couscous is made from both wheat flour and semolina. It has a ball shape and is toasted rather than dried, which gives it a nuttier flavor and chewier texture.

Farro: Farro is a chewy whole grain that is similar in size and shape to rice. It has a golden brown color and nuttier taste. It's an excellent source of protein and fiber, making it a great addition to salads and side dishes.

Green lentils: Green lentils, also known as French green lentils or Puy lentils, are small and glossy and have a nutty flavor. They have the longest cooking time, about 45 minutes, but they remain firm and are perfect or salads and pilafs.

BROWN LENTILS AND BULGUR WITH CRISPY ONIONS

NUT FREE ✦ VEGAN

PREP TIME: 5 MINUTES • COOK TIME: 1 HOUR • SERVES 6

This dish is packed with protein, iron, fiber, and other nutrients and will easily feed a family of four for less than five dollars. It is similar to the Kushari (page 106) but is much simpler in its preparation. My mom used to make this on laundry day as a quick and easy dinner. Now I sell it in my restaurant—and it's one of my most popular dishes! I first made this dish for a vegan customer and gave samples to anyone who was interested. To my happy surprise everyone loved it so much I made it part of my menu.

½ cup olive oil

2 yellow onions, thinly sliced

1 teaspoon salt, divided

1 pound dried brown lentils, rinsed and picked over for debris

8 cups water

1½ cups coarse bulgur #3

1. Line a plate with paper towels and set aside.
2. In a medium saucepan over medium heat, heat the olive oil.
3. Season the onions with ¼ teaspoon of salt and gently drop them into the hot oil. Cook for 7 to 10 minutes until crispy and golden brown, stirring often. Using a slotted spoon, transfer the onions to the prepared plate and set aside. Turn off the heat and let the oil cool.
4. Add the lentils to the cooled oil, along with the water and remaining ¾ teaspoon of salt. Turn the heat to high and bring the mixture to a boil. Lower the heat to medium and cook for about 15 minutes until the lentils are cooked but still firm. Make sure you have about 3 cups of cooking liquid remaining after boiling the lentils. If not, add more water to the pot.

5. Add the bulgur, stir, and return the mixture to a boil. Taste the water and season with more salt, as needed. Turn the heat to low, cover the pan, and cook for 20 minutes. Turn off the heat and let rest, covered, for 10 minutes.
6. Spoon the lentils and bulgur onto a serving platter, top with the crispy onions, and serve.

PER SERVING: CALORIES: 545; TOTAL FAT: 18G; SATURATED FAT: 3G; CARBOHYDRATES: 75G; FIBER: 30G; PROTEIN: 24G; SODIUM: 62MG

SERVING TIP: Serve this dish with Tzatziki Sauce (page 144) but note that it will no longer be vegan.

RAISIN AND CHICKPEA PILAF

GLUTEN FREE ✦ NUT FREE ✦ VEGAN

PREP TIME: 15 MINUTES • COOK TIME: 30 MINUTES • SERVES 4

Historians believe that pilaf was first made in India, sometime after the importation of rice to the Indus River Valley. It is believed that the earliest form of the modern word "pilaf" is the Indo Aryan word *pula*, which means "dish of rice and meat." In this recipe, instead of including meat, we substitute sweet raisins, apricots, and hearty chickpeas.

¼ cup olive oil

½ teaspoon ground turmeric

½ teaspoon ground cardamom

4½ cups water

2 cups basmati rice

1 cup raisins

½ cup chopped dried apricots

1 cup cooked chickpeas

⅛ teaspoon salt, plus more as needed

1. In a heavy-bottomed pot over medium heat, heat the olive oil.
2. Add the turmeric and cardamom. Cook, stirring, for 15 to 20 seconds. Add the water and bring to a boil.
3. Stir in the rice, raisins, apricots, chickpeas, and salt. Taste and season with more salt, as needed.
4. Return the mixture to a boil. Reduce the heat to low, cover the pot, and simmer for 15 minutes.
5. Turn off the heat and let the pilaf rest, covered, for 10 minutes. Fluff with a fork before serving.

PER SERVING: CALORIES: 607; TOTAL FAT: 18G; SATURATED FAT: 2G; CARBOHYDRATES: 112G; FIBER: 9G; PROTEIN: 12G; SODIUM: 81MG

SUBSTITUTION TIP: Use any dried fruits you have in your pantry—dried dates and cranberries work especially well.

LENTIL RAGOUT

GLUTEN FREE ✦ NUT FREE ✦ VEGAN

PREP TIME: 15 MINUTES • COOK TIME: 50 MINUTES • SERVES 6

A ragout is essentially a French variation of a stew. Although usually made with meat and vegetables, my tasty version is made with lentils, which are low in calories, rich in iron and folate, and an excellent source of protein. Serve this with garlic bread for wiping the bowl clean, or use it as a hearty meat-sauce alternative over your favorite noodles.

¼ cup olive oil

1 onion, finely chopped

4 carrots, peeled and cut into ¼-inch dice

2 celery stalks, cut into ¼-inch-thick slices

4 garlic cloves, mashed

1 pound dried French green lentils, rinsed and picked over for debris

4 thyme sprigs

2 bay leaves

½ teaspoon dried oregano

½ teaspoon cayenne pepper

⅛ teaspoon salt

⅛ teaspoon freshly ground black pepper

4 cups vegetable broth

2 tablespoons red wine vinegar

1. In a heavy-bottomed pot over medium heat, heat the olive oil.
2. Add the onion and cook for 5 minutes.
3. Add the carrots, celery, and garlic and cook, stirring often, for 10 minutes more.
4. Stir in the lentils, thyme, bay leaves, oregano, cayenne, salt, black pepper, and vegetable broth. Increase the heat and bring the mixture to a boil. Reduce the heat to medium-low and cook, uncovered, for 30 minutes or until the lentils are tender.
5. Remove and discard the thyme and bay leaves. Stir in the vinegar and serve.

PER SERVING: CALORIES: 379; TOTAL FAT: 9G; SATURATED FAT: 1G; CARBOHYDRATES: 54G; FIBER: 25G; PROTEIN: 20G; SODIUM: 182MG

VARIATION TIP: Use 1 cup pearl onions, 4 baby zucchini, halved, and 8 ounces baby carrots instead of the large vegetables.

FUL MEDAMES

30 MINUTES OR LESS ✦ GLUTEN FREE ✦ NUT FREE ✦ VEGAN

PREP TIME: 15 MINUTES • COOK TIME: 15 MINUTES • SERVES 6

Ful medames is a dish of boiled fava beans mixed with chopped vegetables and warming spices. When you eat ful medames your brain goes into lazy mode. You just want to sit down and go to sleep. For this reason, my mom never served the dish during finals week at school. I suggest you serve this dish with warm Pita Bread (page 152) and drink hot black tea after the meal; it seems to ease the digestion.

1 (15-ounce) can fava beans, undrained

4 garlic cloves, minced

1 tablespoon ground cumin

⅛ teaspoon salt

⅛ teaspoon freshly ground black pepper

½ cup freshly squeezed lemon juice

¼ cup olive oil

1 sweet onion, chopped, divided

2 ripe tomatoes, diced, divided

2 cups finely chopped fresh parsley, divided

1. In a medium saucepan over medium heat, combine the fava beans with their liquid, garlic, cumin, salt, and pepper. Bring to a boil.
2. Using a potato masher or fork, partially mash the fava beans. Continue to cook over medium heat for 10 minutes more.
3. Stir in the lemon juice, olive oil, and half each of the onion, tomatoes, and parsley. Taste and season with more salt and pepper, as needed. Remove from the heat.
4. Spoon the bean mixture into a serving dish and top while hot with the remaining onion, tomatoes, and parsley.

PER SERVING: CALORIES: 183; TOTAL FAT: 9G; SATURATED FAT: 2G; CARBOHYDRATES: 20G; FIBER: 6G; PROTEIN: 7G; SODIUM: 74MG

SWISS CHARD AND BLACK-EYED PEA PILAF

NUT FREE ✦ VEGAN

PREP TIME: 20 MINUTES • COOK TIME: 50 MINUTES • SERVES 4

Did you ever wonder how Swiss chard got its name? Apparently it was first identified by a Swiss botanist. We're lucky he discovered it because it's a nutrient powerhouse high in antioxidants, iron, fiber, and vitamins A, C, and K. One of the farmers I work with plants a lot of Swiss chard and will often bring his bounty to me. There's so much that I chop it, blanch it, and freeze it in small bags to save for future use. I highly recommend you do the same; that way, in winter, you can use it in soups and stews—and to make this healthy dish.

10 cups water, divided

1 pound Swiss chard, or kale, chopped

¼ cup olive oil

1 onion, chopped

1 cup canned black-eyed peas, drained and rinsed (see tip)

1 garlic clove, mashed

½ teaspoon ground coriander

1 cup coarse bulgur #3

1. In a large soup pot over medium heat, bring 8 cups of water to a boil. Add the Swiss chard and return it to a boil. Cook for 5 minutes. Remove from the heat, drain, and set aside to cool.
2. Return the soup pot to medium heat and add the olive oil to warm.
3. Add the onion and cook for 5 minutes. Add the black-eyed peas and cook for 10 minutes more. Stir in the garlic, coriander, and Swiss chard. Cook for 1 minute.
4. Pour the remaining 2 cups of water over the vegetables, increase the heat, and bring the mixture to a boil.
5. Add the bulgur and return everything to a boil. Reduce the heat to medium-low, cover the pot, and cook for 10 minutes. Turn off the heat and let the pilaf rest for 10 minutes before serving.

PER SERVING: CALORIES: 307; TOTAL FAT: 14G; SATURATED FAT: 2G; CARBOHYDRATES: 42G; FIBER: 11G; PROTEIN: 10G; SODIUM: 262MG

SUBSTITUTION TIP: You can use frozen black-eyed peas, but thaw them before cooking.

SPICED LENTILS WITH DUMPLINGS

NUT FREE ✦ VEGAN

PREP TIME: 20 MINUTES • COOK TIME: 40 MINUTES • SERVES 8

The name for this dish in Arabic translates to "burn your fingers." To make the dumplings, you drop small balls of dough into the hot lentil stew, and I bet more than one cook probably burned their fingers doing so. But don't let this scare you. Drop the dough with a spoon instead and your fingers will be fine—and you can use the spoon to taste test!

1 cup olive oil

2 large onions, thinly sliced

2 cups chopped fresh cilantro

6 garlic cloves, minced

1 tablespoon ground coriander

1 tablespoon ground cumin

1 pound dried brown lentils, rinsed and picked over for debris

10 cups water

⅛ teaspoon salt

⅛ teaspoon freshly ground black pepper

1 cup pomegranate molasses, or aged balsamic vinegar

½ cup freshly squeezed lemon juice

½ yield Pita Bread dough (page 152), or 3 (4-inch) balls store-bought pizza dough

½ cup all-purpose flour

1. Line a plate with paper towels and set aside.
2. In a large soup pot or Dutch oven over medium heat, heat the olive oil.
3. Add the onions and fry for about 10 minutes until golden and crispy. Using a slotted spoon, transfer the onions to the prepared plate to drain.
4. Add the cilantro, garlic, coriander, and cumin to the oil. Stir and cook for 1 minute. Transfer half the herb mixture to a plate and set aside.
5. Add the lentils, water, salt, and pepper to the remaining herb mixture in the pot. Bring to a boil and cook for about 20 minutes until the lentils are done.
6. Stir in the molasses and lemon juice.
7. Portion the dough into ½-inch balls. Dust them with the flour and drop them into the cooking lentils. Cook for 5 minutes.
8. Spoon the lentils and dumplings onto a shallow serving platter. Spread the reserved herb mixture over the lentils, top with the crispy onions, and enjoy.

PER SERVING: CALORIES: 580; TOTAL FAT: 27G; SATURATED FAT: 4G; CARBOHYDRATES: 66G; FIBER: 20G; PROTEIN: 20G; SODIUM: 199MG

LENTIL AND MUSHROOM LASAGNA

NUT FREE

PREP TIME: 20 MINUTES • COOK TIME: 40 MINUTES • SERVES 4

My husband and I fell in love with this dish when we had it at a neighborhood restaurant in Rome. My husband even asked the owner for the recipe and ended up buying 15 pounds of Italian lentils to bring home to the United States so I could cook this dish for him. In addition to seeing the look on the custom official's face when he saw the lentils, we get to enjoy this incredible dish at home—and now you can, too!

2 cups dried brown lentils, rinsed and picked over for debris

6 cups water

¼ cup olive oil

1 onion, finely chopped

4 garlic cloves, minced

1 pound white mushrooms, cut into slices

½ cup chopped fresh cilantro

4 cups Basic Tomato Basil Sauce (page 145), or store-bought, divided

⅛ teaspoon salt, plus more as needed

⅛ teaspoon freshly ground black pepper, plus more as needed

1 (9-ounce) package no-boil lasagna sheets

1 cup shredded fresh mozzarella cheese

1. Preheat the oven to 400°F.
2. In a large saucepan over high heat, combine the lentils and water. Bring to a boil. Reduce the heat to medium-low and cook for about 10 minutes until the lentils are tender but not mushy. Drain and set aside.
3. In a sauté pan or skillet over medium heat, heat the olive oil.
4. Add the onion and cook for 5 minutes. Stir in the garlic, mushrooms, and cilantro. Cook for 5 minutes.
5. Stir in the lentils, 2 cups of tomato sauce, the salt, and pepper. Taste and season with more salt and pepper, as needed. Remove from the heat.
6. Spoon and spread 1 cup of tomato sauce over the bottom of a 9-by-13-inch baking dish. Cover the sauce with a layer of lasagna sheets.
7. Spoon and spread the lentil mixture evenly over the lasagna. Cover the lentils with a layer of lasagna sheets. Pour the remaining 1 cup of tomato sauce over the lasagna sheets.
8. Bake for 15 minutes. Sprinkle with the mozzarella cheese and bake for 5 minutes more or until the cheese is browned and bubbling.

PER SERVING: CALORIES: 810; TOTAL FAT: 22G; SATURATED FAT: 6G; CARBOHYDRATES: 117G; FIBER: 16G; PROTEIN: 45G; SODIUM: 270MG

FARRO WITH MUSHROOMS AND SCALLIONS

PREP TIME: 20 MINUTES • SOAK TIME: 1 HOUR
COOK TIME: 1 HOUR, 10 MINUTES • SERVES 6

Farro is an ancient grain considered to be a cousin of wheat, which means it's not gluten free. Once seemingly forgotten, this nutrient-packed grain is having a bit of a resurgence. I can even find it in our local grocery store in South Dakota. It has a nutty flavor, a chewy bite, and is full of fiber and protein. Sometimes when I add cooked farro to my salads people will ask if there are crushed cashews in it—so I add it to anything that could use a bit of flavor and texture.

1½ cups dried farro

Hot water, for soaking the farro

½ cup olive oil

1 onion, finely chopped

1 pound mixed shiitake and cremini mushrooms, cleaned and cut into slices

1 garlic clove, minced

⅛ teaspoon salt, plus more as needed

½ cup dry white wine, or vegetable broth

3 cups vegetable broth

¼ cup chopped fresh oregano

½ cup chopped scallions, white and green parts

2 tablespoons pine nuts, toasted

Shaved Parmesan cheese, for serving (optional)

1. Place the farro in a bowl, cover it with hot water, and let soak for 1 hour.
2. In a heavy-bottomed skillet over medium-low heat, heat the olive oil. Add the onion and cook for about 5 minutes until golden.
3. Add the mushrooms, garlic, and salt. Cook for about 5 minutes, stirring often, until tender.
4. Drain the farro and add it to the onion and mushrooms. Cook for 2 minutes.
5. Stir in the wine and cook for about 15 minutes until the liquid has been absorbed.
6. Add the vegetable broth and oregano and bring to a boil. Taste and season with more salt, as needed. Reduce the heat to low, cover the skillet, and cook for 30 minutes. Remove from the heat but let sit, covered, for 10 minutes more.
7. Spoon the farro onto a serving platter. Sprinkle with the scallions and pine nuts and top with the Parmesan cheese (if using) just before serving.

PER SERVING: CALORIES: 338; TOTAL FAT: 20G; SATURATED FAT: 3G; CARBOHYDRATES: 30G; FIBER: 7G; PROTEIN: 8G; SODIUM: 158MG

BUTTERNUT SQUASH, ZUCCHINI, AND BULGUR PILAF

VEGAN

PREP TIME: 25 MINUTES • COOK TIME: 50 MINUTES • SERVES 4

Once upon a time, my mother would make bulgur with zucchini, and everyone would complain. It wasn't a very popular dish in our household. Recently, one of the farmers I work with gave me a case of butternut squash, and I decided to make my mom's dish—with a bit of modification. The creamy butternut squash is a great complement to the chewiness of the bulgur, the crunch of the walnuts, and the zesty kick of jalapeño.

3 pounds butternut squash, peeled, seeded, and cut into ½-inch-thick half-moons

¼ cup olive oil, divided

1 small onion, finely chopped

4 scallions, white and green parts, chopped

1 zucchini, diced

1 jalapeño pepper, seeded and finely chopped

½ red bell pepper, chopped

2 tomatoes, diced

¼ cup chopped fresh cilantro

½ cup coarse bulgur #3

¼ cup coarsely chopped walnuts

1. Preheat the oven to 400°F.
2. On a baking sheet, toss together the butternut squash and 1 tablespoon of olive oil until coated. Spread into a single layer. Bake for 10 minutes. Remove and set aside.
3. In a large skillet over medium heat, heat the remaining 3 tablespoons of olive oil.
4. Add the onion and cook for 5 minutes. Add the scallions, zucchini, jalapeño, red bell pepper, tomatoes, and cilantro. Toss to coat. Reduce the heat to medium-low and cook for 10 minutes.
5. Stir in the bulgur and bring the mixture to a boil. Reduce the heat to low, cover the skillet, and cook for 15 minutes.
6. Remove the skillet from the heat, stir in the butternut squash and walnuts, cover, and let the pilaf rest for 10 minutes before serving.

PER SERVING: CALORIES: 408; TOTAL FAT: 18G; SATURATED FAT: 3G; CARBOHYDRATES: 62G; FIBER: 13G; PROTEIN: 8G; SODIUM: 28MG

MOROCCAN-STYLE VEGETABLE AND OLIVE TAGINE

GLUTEN FREE ✦ NUT FREE

PREP TIME: 25 MINUTES • COOK TIME: 50 MINUTES • SERVES 6

The word *tagine* refers to the earthenware pot in which the stew is cooked. The tagine's cone-shaped lid traps the steam rising from the juicy, delicious food inside, infusing the dish with amazing flavors. If you do not have a tagine, a Dutch oven will work fine. You can even cover the lid of your regular cooking pot in aluminum foil for a tighter fit to trap the steam and harness the aromas of this classic dish.

½ cup olive oil

1 onion, chopped

2 celery stalks, chopped

1 (32-ounce) can diced tomatoes

4 cups water

4 garlic cloves, slivered

2 bay leaves

Grated zest of 1 lemon

1 teaspoon chopped fresh thyme

⅛ teaspoon salt, plus more as needed

8 ounces baby potatoes, halved

2 carrots, peeled and cut into 1-inch matchsticks

1 fennel bulb, quartered, white parts only (see tip)

1. In a Dutch oven or tagine over medium heat, heat the olive oil.
2. Add the onion and celery and cook for 5 minutes.
3. Stir in the tomatoes, water, garlic, bay leaves, lemon zest, thyme, and salt. Taste and season with more salt, as needed. Bring the mixture to a boil. Reduce the heat to low and simmer for 5 minutes.
4. Add the potatoes, carrots, and fennel. Increase the heat to return the mixture to a boil. Reduce the heat to medium-low, cover the pot, and cook for 20 minutes.
5. When the vegetables are almost done cooking, melt the ghee in a small skillet over medium heat. Stir in the cumin, coriander, and pepper. Cook for 30 seconds. Stir in the lemon juice.
6. Stir the spice mixture into the stew, along with the chickpeas and olives. Cover the pot, increase the heat to medium, and cook for 5 minutes more.
7. Turn off the heat and let the tagine rest, covered, for 10 minutes before serving.

2 tablespoons Ghee
(page 148), or butter

½ teaspoon ground cumin

½ teaspoon ground coriander

½ teaspoon freshly ground
black pepper

¼ cup freshly squeezed
lemon juice

1 (15-ounce) can chickpeas,
drained and rinsed

½ cup pitted green olives

PER SERVING: CALORIES: 346; TOTAL FAT: 24G; SATURATED FAT: 5G;
CARBOHYDRATES: 31G; FIBER: 9G; PROTEIN: 7G; SODIUM: 267MG

INGREDIENT TIP: Fennel is a bulb vegetable very popular
around the Mediterranean region. When buying fennel, look for a
large, tight, white bulb free of bruises. Check the fronds or feath-
ers to ensure there are no signs of a flower head, which signals
the fennel has passed its prime.

SUBSTITUTION TIP: Skip the ghee or butter for a vegan dish.

CHAPTER 6
PASTAS, PIZZAS, AND BREADS

FRESH SAUCE PASTA

30 MINUTES OR LESS ✦ NUT FREE

PREP TIME: 15 MINUTES • COOK TIME: 15 MINUTES • SERVES 4

It's hard to believe a recipe this simple can be so tasty. This is one of my favorite ways to use the abundance of tomatoes in my garden during summer months. I suggest sprinkling Parmesan cheese over your pasta before serving, but a sprinkle of goat cheese adds a wonderful new layer of flavors, if you like.

⅛ teaspoon salt, plus more for cooking the pasta

1 pound penne pasta

¼ cup olive oil

1 garlic clove, crushed

3 cups chopped scallions, white and green parts

3 tomatoes, diced

2 tablespoons chopped fresh basil

⅛ teaspoon freshly ground black pepper

Freshly grated Parmesan cheese, for serving

1. Bring a large pot of salted water to a boil over high heat. Drop in the pasta, stir, and return the water to a boil. Boil the pasta for about 6 minutes or until al dente.
2. A couple minutes before the pasta is completely cooked, in a medium saucepan over medium heat, heat the olive oil.
3. Add the garlic and cook for 30 seconds.
4. Stir in the scallions and tomatoes. Cover the pan and cook for 2 to 3 minutes.
5. Drain the pasta and add it to the vegetables. Stir in the basil and season with the salt and pepper. Top with the Parmesan cheese.

PER SERVING: CALORIES: 477; TOTAL FAT: 16G; SATURATED FAT: 2G; CARBOHYDRATES: 72G; FIBER: 3G; PROTEIN: 15G; SODIUM: 120MG

THREE SAUCES LASAGNA

FREEZER FRIENDLY ✦ NUT FREE

PREP TIME: 30 MINUTES • COOK TIME: 45 MINUTES • SERVES 8

Contrary to common belief, lasagna did not originate in Italy; it came to us from ancient Greece. The word "lasagna" is derived from the Greek word *laganon*, the first known form of pasta. This dish is one of my daughter's favorite meals and we make it together whenever she visits. I layer the lasagna sheets and she spoons the sauce over them—she loves basil so she always spoons on extra pesto.

1 cup ricotta

1 cup Basil Pesto (page 141), or store-bought

4 cups Basic Tomato Basil Sauce (page 145), or store-bought, divided

2 (9-ounce) packages no-boil lasagna sheets

4 cups Béchamel Sauce (page 146), divided

½ cup freshly grated Parmesan cheese

VARIATION TIP: Add cooked spinach or other cooked vegetables as an extra layer.

MAKE AHEAD: Prepare in advance and freeze for up to 1 month. When ready to bake, thaw in the refrigerator overnight and bake for 40 minutes in a 375°F oven or until cooked through.

1. Preheat the oven to 375°F.
2. In a small mixing bowl, stir together the ricotta and pesto. Set aside.
3. Spread 1 cup of tomato sauce on the bottom of a 9-by-13-inch baking dish. Cover the sauce with a few lasagna sheets.
4. Spread 2 cups of béchamel sauce evenly on top of the lasagna sheets. Cover with a few more lasagna sheets.
5. Spread the ricotta and pesto mixture evenly over the lasagna sheets.
6. Pour 1 cup of tomato sauce over the ricotta layer and cover the sauce with a few lasagna sheets.
7. Spread the remaining 2 cups of béchamel sauce over the lasagna sheets. Cover with a few more lasagna sheets.
8. Pour the remaining 2 cups of tomato sauce over the sheets. Top with the Parmesan cheese.
9. Bake for 30 minutes or until the cheese on top is melted and golden brown. Let rest for 15 minutes before serving.

PER SERVING: CALORIES: 616; TOTAL FAT: 27G; SATURATED FAT: 10G; CARBOHYDRATES: 71G; FIBER: 4G; PROTEIN: 16G; SODIUM: 537MG

TORTELLINI IN MINT YOGURT SAUCE

FREEZER FRIENDLY ✦ NUT FREE

PREP TIME: 15 MINUTES • COOK TIME: 25 MINUTES • SERVES 6

Tortellini is called *shish barak* in the Middle East, and usually they are filled with ground lamb meat and pine nuts. In this recipe mushrooms replace the lamb. Traditionally, the dough for shish barak is basic pita dough. My mom would get my sister and me to help her prepare this dish: One would flatten the dough, one would cut the dough into 3-inch rounds, and then my mom would stuff and fold it into a hat shape. In this recipe I use store-bought mushroom-stuffed tortellini so you can enjoy without two extra sets of hands. If you don't like mushrooms, buy any kind of vegetarian tortellini you like.

¼ cup cornstarch

1 cup cold water

6 cups Plain Yogurt (page 150), or store-bought

¼ teaspoon ground nutmeg

½ teaspoon salt, plus more as needed

2 tablespoons Ghee (page 148), butter, or olive oil

3 garlic cloves, minced

1 tablespoon dried mint

1 pound store-bought mushroom-filled tortellini, cooked according to the package directions

1. In a large bowl, whisk the cornstarch and cold water until the cornstarch dissolves. Add the yogurt and whisk well. Place a fine-mesh sieve over a medium saucepan and pour the yogurt mixture through the sieve to remove any lumps.
2. Stir in the nutmeg and salt. Taste and season with more salt, as needed. Place the pan over medium heat and cook, stirring continuously, for about 20 minutes or until the sauce thickens and begins to coat the back of a spoon.
3. In a small saucepan over medium heat, melt the ghee.
4. Add the garlic to the ghee and cook for 1 minute. Stir in the mint, remove from the heat, and stir the mixture into the yogurt sauce. Taste and adjust the seasoning.
5. Add the cooked tortellini to the yogurt sauce, stirring so they are coated. Cook over low heat for 5 minutes or until heated through.

PER SERVING: CALORIES: 413; TOTAL FAT: 19G; SATURATED FAT: 10G; CARBOHYDRATES: 45G; FIBER: 4G; PROTEIN: 17G; SODIUM: 493MG

HOMEMADE SHISH BARAK

FREEZER FRIENDLY ✦ NUT FREE ✦ VEGAN

PREP TIME: 40 MINUTES • COOK TIME: 20 MINUTES
MAKES 40 DUMPLINGS

¼ cup olive oil

1 onion, chopped

1 pound white
  mushrooms, chopped

1 garlic clove, mashed

½ teaspoon salt

½ teaspoon freshly
  ground black pepper

All-purpose flour,
  for dusting

Pita Bread dough
  (page 152)

1. In a medium sauté pan or skillet over medium heat, heat the olive oil.
2. Add the onion and cook for about 5 minutes until golden. Add the mushrooms and cook for about 10 minutes until their natural water evaporates, stirring often.
3. Stir in the garlic, salt, and pepper. Remove from the heat.
4. Preheat the oven to 350°F.
5. Dust a work surface with flour and roll out the pita dough on it to ⅛ inch thick. Using a 2-inch round glass or cookie cutter, cut rounds from the dough.
6. Place ½ teaspoon of mushroom stuffing in the center of each dough circle. Fold the circle in half and pinch the edges together to form a hat-like shape. Place the tortellini on a baking sheet.
7. Bake for 5 minutes.
8. Let cool. Once cooled, use them in the Tortellini in Mint Yogurt Sauce (page 126) or freeze in a freezer bag for up to 3 months.

PER SERVING: CALORIES: 413; TOTAL FAT: 19G; SATURATED FAT: 10G; CARBOHYDRATES: 45G; FIBER: 4G; PROTEIN: 17G; SODIUM: 493MG

PENNE IN TOMATO AND CAPER SAUCE

30 MINUTES OR LESS ✦ NUT FREE ✦ VEGAN

PREP TIME: 10 MINUTES • COOK TIME: 15 MINUTES • SERVES 4

Capers are the unripened flower buds of the caper bush, a plant native to the Mediterranean. Capers are often preserved by pickling them in salt and vinegar brine. Although pasta with tomato sauce is delicious, adding capers takes it to another flavor level. I keep a jar of capers in my refrigerator ready to use in this dish.

2 tablespoons olive oil

2 garlic cloves, minced

1 cup sliced cherry tomatoes

2 cups Basic Tomato Basil Sauce (page 145), or store-bought

1 cup capers, drained and rinsed

Salt

4 cups penne pasta

1. Set a large pot of salted water over high heat to boil.
2. In a medium saucepan over medium heat, heat the olive oil. Add the garlic and cook for 30 seconds. Add the cherry tomatoes and cook for 2 to 3 minutes.
3. Pour in the tomato sauce and bring the mixture to a boil. Stir in the capers and turn off the heat.
4. Once boiling add the pasta to the pot of water and cook for about 7 minutes until al dente.
5. Drain the pasta and stir it into the sauce. Toss gently and cook over medium heat for 1 minute or until warmed through.

PER SERVING: CALORIES: 329; TOTAL FAT: 8G; SATURATED FAT: 1G; CARBOHYDRATES: 55G; FIBER: 6G; PROTEIN: 10G; SODIUM: 612MG

SERVING TIP: Serve this dish topped with shaved or grated Parmesan cheese; just note it will no longer be vegan.

VARIATION TIP: Add ½ cup chopped pitted green olives for a simple pasta puttanesca.

SPAGHETTI PESTO CAKE

PREP TIME: 10 MINUTES • COOK TIME: 40 MINUTES • SERVES 6

This dish is a savory take on cake! I love it because it's really versatile and can easily be changed accommodate different food sensitivities without sacrificing flavor. See the tip below to learn how I make this dish for my vegan customers. I recommend topping the cake with Basic Tomato Basil Sauce (page 145), if you like.

12 ounces ricotta

1 cup Basil Pesto (page 141), or store-bought

2 tablespoons olive oil

¼ cup freshly grated Parmesan cheese

Salt

1 pound spaghetti

1. Preheat the oven to 400°F. Set a large pot of salted water to boil over high heat.
2. In a food processor, combine the ricotta and basil pesto. Purée into a smooth cream and transfer to a large bowl. Set aside.
3. Coat a 10-cup Bundt pan with the olive oil and sprinkle with the Parmesan cheese. Set aside.
4. Once the water is boiling, add the pasta to the pot and cook for about 6 minutes until al dente.
5. Drain the pasta well and add it to the pesto cream. Mix well until all the pasta is saturated with the sauce.
6. Spoon the pasta into the prepared pan, pressing to ensure it is tightly packed. Bake for 30 minutes.
7. Place a flat serving platter on top of the cake pan. Quickly and carefully invert the pasta cake. Gently remove the pan. Cut into slices and serve topped with your favorite sauce, if desired.

PER SERVING: CALORIES: 622; TOTAL FAT: 30G; SATURATED FAT: 7G; CARBOHYDRATES: 67G; FIBER: 3G; PROTEIN: 20G; SODIUM: 425MG

SUBSTITUTION TIP: For a dairy-free version of this cake: Purée 12 ounces firm tofu, 2 cups chopped fresh basil, 6 peeled garlic cloves, ½ teaspoon salt, and ½ cup olive oil into a smooth paste. Then follow steps 3 through 7 (just coat the pan with flour rather than Parmesan).

MARGHERITA PIZZA

NUT FREE

PREP TIME: 10 MINUTES • RISE TIME: 1 HOUR • COOK TIME: 10 MINUTES • SERVES 4

Around the Mediterranean, pizza is just dough covered with a little sauce, a bit of cheese, and a few vegetables. Nowhere will you find stuffed-crust pizza, pineapple pizza, or extra-meat pizza. At home, I spread za'atar and olive oil over the dough, crumble a little goat cheese on top, and sprinkle with diced tomato. My husband loves red onion and mushroom on his pizza. You can skip the cheese and just spread it with Basil Pesto (page 141), top with fresh tomato slices, and bake. The variety is as wide as your imagination.

1 tablespoon olive oil

½ yield Pizza Dough
(page 153), or
1 pound store-bought

8 ounces fresh mozzarella
cheese, cut into 1-inch cubes

All-purpose flour, for dusting

1 teaspoon cornmeal

1 cup Basic Tomato Basil
Sauce (page 145),
or store-bought

½ cup chopped fresh
basil, divided

1 tablespoon freshly grated
Parmesan cheese

1. Coat a medium bowl with the olive oil. Place the dough in the bowl, cover with a clean kitchen towel, and let rise for 1 hour or until the dough doubles in size.
2. Preheat the oven to 500°F.
3. Pat the mozzarella cheese dry with paper towels.
4. Dust a work surface with flour and turn the dough out onto it. Flatten the dough into a 10-inch circle. Sprinkle the cornmeal on a baking sheet. Place the dough circle on the baking sheet.
5. Spread the tomato sauce on the pizza, leaving a ½-inch border all around. Scatter the mozzarella and half the basil over the sauce.
6. Bake for about 10 minutes until the crust is golden and the cheese is bubbling.
7. Sprinkle with the remaining basil and the Parmesan cheese. Serve hot!

PER SERVING: CALORIES: 460; TOTAL FAT: 24G; SATURATED FAT: 9G; CARBOHYDRATES: 45G; FIBER: 7G; PROTEIN: 22G; SODIUM: 391MG

NO-KNEAD SESAME BREAD

NUT FREE

PREP TIME: 20 MINUTES • RISE TIME: 1 HOUR, 30 MINUTES
COOK TIME: 10 MINUTES • MAKES 2 LOAVES

This Turkish bread is topped with both white and black sesame seeds and leaves plenty of room for customization. For a different savory flavor, try spreading harissa (page 143) over the dough before sprinkling on the sesame seeds.

3 tablespoons olive oil, divided

½ yield Pita Bread dough (page 152)

¼ cup all-purpose flour, for dusting

1 large egg yolk

¼ cup milk

1 tablespoon white sesame seeds

1 tablespoon black sesame seeds

1. Coat 2 baking sheets with 1 tablespoon of olive oil each and set aside.
2. Coat a large bowl with the remaining 1 tablespoon of olive oil. Place the dough in the bowl, cover with a clean kitchen towel, and let rise for 1 hour or until the dough doubles in size.
3. Dust a work surface with flour and turn the dough out on to it. Cut the dough into 2 balls. Keep dusting with flour to prevent sticking. Roll out the balls into ½-inch-thick flat circles. Place each dough circle on a prepared baking sheet. Cover and let rest for 30 minutes.
4. Preheat the oven to 450°F.
5. In a small bowl, whisk the egg yolk and milk until combined. Set aside.
6. Using your fingertips, dent the tops of the dough all over. Brush the dough with the egg-and-milk glaze. Sprinkle 1½ teaspoons each of white and black sesame seeds over each dough circle.
7. Bake for about 10 minutes or until the edges begin to brown. Serve warm.

PER SERVING: (½ LOAF) CALORIES: 338; TOTAL FAT: 18G; SATURATED FAT: 3G; CARBOHYDRATES: 38G; FIBER: 3G; PROTEIN: 8G; SODIUM: 303MG

CHEESE AND PARSLEY FLATBREAD

NUT FREE

PREP TIME: 25 MINUTES • RISE TIME: 10 MINUTES • COOK TIME: 25 MINUTES • SERVES 4

These delicious flatbreads are packed with protein, making them an excellent snack. I used to pack them in my daughter's school lunch bag—and now that she's in college, I make them, freeze them, and ship them to her!

1 cup crumbled feta cheese

1 large egg

½ cup finely chopped fresh parsley

⅛ teaspoon freshly ground black pepper

½ yield Pita Bread dough (page 152)

All-purpose flour, for dusting

2 tablespoons olive oil

½ teaspoon black sesame seeds

1. In a medium bowl, stir together the feta cheese, egg, parsley, and pepper. Set aside.
2. Divide the pita dough into 4 balls. Dust each with flour and place each dough ball into a bowl. Cover and let rise for 10 minutes.
3. Dust a work surface with flour. Punch down each dough ball and roll them out into 3-by-12-inch ovals.
4. Preheat the oven to 400°F.
5. Spread a quarter of the feta filling on each piece of dough. Pinch the top and bottom of each bread, and fold the sides inward to create a boat shape. Brush the dough with olive oil and sprinkle with the sesame seeds.
6. Bake for 12 to 15 minutes or until golden. Let cool for 10 minutes before serving.

PER SERVING: CALORIES: 335; TOTAL FAT: 18G; SATURATED FAT: 7G; CARBOHYDRATES: 32G; FIBER: 2G; PROTEIN: 12G; SODIUM: 653MG

VARIATION TIP: Mix the feta cheese with 1 cup ricotta, ½ cup chopped green olives, and ½ teaspoon dried oregano for a different take.

FLATBREAD WITH HARISSA AND SESAME

NUT FREE ✦ VEGAN

PREP TIME: 25 MINUTES • RISE TIME: 15 MINUTES • COOK TIME: 15 MINUTES • SERVES 4

In the Mediterranean, this classic loaf is typically baked to order. You can stop at the bakery window, place your order, and do some more shopping while you wait. This combination is one of my favorites.

½ yield Pita Bread dough (page 152)

All-purpose flour, for dusting

¼ cup olive oil

1 small onion, finely chopped

¼ cup Harissa (page 143), or store-bought

2 tablespoons sesame seeds

1. Cut the dough into 2 equal balls. Dust a work surface with flour, place the balls on the flour, cover, and let rise for 15 minutes.
2. In a small sauté pan or skillet over medium heat, heat the olive oil.
3. Add the onion and cook for about 5 minutes until transparent. Remove from the heat and stir in the harissa. Set aside.
4. Preheat the oven to 400°F.
5. Roll out each dough ball into an 8-inch circle, dusting with flour as needed to prevent sticking. Transfer the dough to a baking sheet.
6. Spread half the onion-harissa mixture over each dough circle and sprinkle each with 1 tablespoon of sesame seeds.
7. Bake for 10 minutes or until the edges are golden.

PER SERVING: CALORIES: 358; TOTAL FAT: 21G; SATURATED FAT: 3G; CARBOHYDRATES: 39G; FIBER: 3G; PROTEIN: 7G; SODIUM: 473MG

VARIATION TIP: Sprinkle with chopped cured black olives and fresh thyme before baking for a different flavor combination.

ROSEMARY FOCACCIA

NUT FREE ✦ VEGAN

PREP TIME: 15 MINUTES • RISE TIME: 50 MINUTES • COOK TIME: 20 MINUTES • SERVES 6

Rosemary is rich in anti-inflammatory compounds, which are thought to help boost the immune system and improve blood circulation. For this reason, as well as its particular flavor, rosemary is an herb often used in Mediterranean cooking. I think you will find it a delightful complement to this bread. For an added treat, top the focaccia with caramelized onions.

½ cup olive oil, divided

1 yield Pizza Dough (page 153), or 2 pounds store-bought

All-purpose flour, for dusting

¼ cup chopped fresh rosemary, plus 1 rosemary sprig

1½ teaspoons salt, divided

¼ cup water

1. Preheat the oven to 400°F.
2. Coat a medium bowl with 1 tablespoon of olive oil. Place the dough in the bowl, cover with a clean kitchen towel, and let rise for 30 minutes.
3. Flour a work surface and turn the dough out on to it. Roll out the dough into a ½-inch-thick rectangle. Transfer the rectangle to a baking sheet.
4. Using your fingertips, make deep dents all over the dough. Drizzle with the remaining 7 tablespoons of olive oil and sprinkle with the chopped rosemary. Let rest for 20 minutes.
5. In a small bowl, stir together 1 teaspoon of salt and the water. Drizzle over the dough. Sprinkle the rosemary needles from the sprig evenly across the dough. Sprinkle on the remaining ½ teaspoon of salt.
6. Bake for 20 minutes or until the dough is slightly golden.

PER SERVING: CALORIES: 450; TOTAL FAT: 25G; SATURATED FAT: 4G; CARBOHYDRATES: 48G; FIBER: 8G; PROTEIN: 8G; SODIUM: 156MG

ZA'ATAR BREAD

30 MINUTES OR LESS ✦ NUT FREE ✦ VEGAN

PREP TIME: 20 MINUTES • RISE TIME: 10 MINUTES • COOK TIME: 15 MINUTES • SERVES 4

Each village around the Eastern Mediterranean makes their own version of za'atar and uses it on breads, salads, and in main dishes. Za'atar is made mainly from wild Mediterranean thyme mixed with sumac, ground toasted chickpeas, and sesame seeds. Some people will add slivered pistachios, coconut flakes, and so on. I think my mom's za'atar is the best. She still ships me a couple kilos every year. This bread tastes great topped with arugula and fresh tomato slices.

¾ cup olive oil

½ cup Sanaa's Za'atar (page 44), or store-bought

All-purpose flour, for dusting

½ yield Pita Bread dough (page 152)

1. In a small bowl, whisk the olive oil and za'atar until combined. Set aside.
2. Dust a work surface with flour. Divide the dough into 4 balls and place them on the flour. Cover and let rise for 10 minutes.
3. Preheat the oven to 450°F.
4. Roll each ball into a ¼-inch-thick round. Transfer the rounds to a baking sheet. Evenly spread the za'atar oil over each round.
5. Bake for 10 minutes or until the edges are golden brown. Let cool for 5 minutes before serving.

PER SERVING: CALORIES: 499; TOTAL FAT: 41G; SATURATED FAT: 5G; CARBOHYDRATES: 30G; FIBER: 3G; PROTEIN: 5G; SODIUM: 333MG

SWEET ANISE BREAD

FREEZER FRIENDLY ✦ NUT FREE

PREP TIME: 20 MINUTES • COOK TIME: 1 HOUR • SERVES 8

Aniseed is native to Eastern Mediterranean countries. The flavor is similar to fennel and licorice. This bread is good for breakfast with apricot jam, as an afternoon snack with a cup of black tea, or with fruit-flavored butter (see the tip on page 149) as an after-dinner dessert. Even better, it can be made in advance and frozen for up to 1 month before use.

2 tablespoons olive oil, plus more for preparing the pan

2 cups all-purpose flour, plus more for dusting

1 cup sugar

1½ teaspoons baking powder

1 teaspoon aniseed

½ teaspoon ground cinnamon

¼ teaspoon salt

1 large egg

½ cup milk

1 tablespoon freshly squeezed orange juice

Grated zest of 1 orange

1. Preheat the oven to 375°F. Coat a 5-by-9-inch loaf pan with olive oil. Set aside.
2. In a medium bowl, whisk the flour, sugar, baking powder, aniseed, cinnamon, and salt. Set aside.
3. In a small bowl, whisk the egg, milk, olive oil, orange juice, and orange zest. Add the egg mixture to the flour mixture and mix until well combined and a smooth dough forms.
4. Dust a work surface with flour. Place the dough on it and flatten the dough to fit into the prepared loaf pan. Place the dough in the pan.
5. Bake for about 50 minutes or until golden. Let the bread rest in the pan for 10 minutes. Transfer to a wire rack to cool completely.

PER SERVING: CALORIES: 257; TOTAL FAT: 5G; SATURATED FAT: 1G; CARBOHYDRATES: 51G; FIBER: 1G; PROTEIN: 5G; SODIUM: 91MG

BRIOCHE

NUT FREE

PREP TIME: 1 HOUR • RISE AND REST TIME: 2 HOURS
COOK TIME: 40 MINUTES • MAKES 1 LOAF

Brioche is a light, puffy, sweet bread. It's delicious plain with a good cup of coffee, but it can also be stuffed with jam or chocolate.

½ cup sugar, divided

1 tablespoon dry active yeast

1 cup warm milk

3 cups all-purpose flour

½ teaspoon salt

3 large eggs, divided

1 cup (2 sticks) unsalted butter, at room temperature, cut into 1-inch pieces, plus more for preparing the pan

½ cup raisins

1 teaspoon aniseed

2 tablespoons water

1. In a small bowl, stir together 1 tablespoon of sugar, the yeast, and milk. Set aside for about 5 minutes until the mixture is frothy.
2. In the bowl of a stand mixer fitted with the dough hook attachment, combine the flour, salt, and remaining 7 tablespoons of sugar. Add the yeast mixture, and stir to combine. Turn the mixer to medium speed.
3. One at a time, add 2 eggs to the flour mixture. Mix for about 15 minutes until a dough begins to form.
4. With the mixer still running, one piece at a time, add the butter to the dough. Continue mixing the dough for 10 minutes until smooth and elastic.
5. Place the dough in a bowl and fold in the raisins and aniseed. Cover and let rise for about 1 hour until it doubles in size. Grease a 5-by-9-inch bread pan with butter.
6. Divide the dough into 3 strands, each 9 inches long. Braid them together, tucking the ends into the braid. Place the bread in the prepared pan, cover, and let rest for 1 hour.
7. Preheat the oven to 350°F.
8. In a small bowl, whisk the remaining egg and the water until combined. Brush the bread with the egg wash. Bake for 40 minutes or until the brioche is golden and glossy.

PER SERVING: (1 SLICE) CALORIES: 328; TOTAL FAT: 17G; SATURATED FAT: 10G; CARBOHYDRATES: 39G; FIBER: 1G; PROTEIN: 6G; SODIUM: 233MG

MEDITERRANEAN STAPLES

TAHINI SAUCE

30 MINUTES OR LESS ✦ GLUTEN FREE ✦ NUT FREE ✦ VEGAN

PREP TIME: 15 MINUTES • MAKES 2 CUPS

As mentioned, sesame seeds are a staple in Mediterranean cuisine, and are used in all kinds of dishes—one of them being tahini, which is used in hummus, savory dishes, and desserts such as halva, an Eastern Mediterranean dessert made of a mixture of tahini, powdered milk, and sugar syrup.

3 garlic cloves, minced or mashed into a paste

½ cup tahini

½ cup freshly squeezed lemon juice

1 cup water

¼ teaspoon ground cumin

⅛ teaspoon salt

In a small bowl, whisk the garlic, tahini, lemon juice, water, cumin, and salt until it develops into a smooth paste. Refrigerate in an airtight container for up to 1 month.

PER SERVING: (1 TABLESPOON) CALORIES: 47; TOTAL FAT: 4G; SATURATED FAT: 1G; CARBOHYDRATES: 2G; FIBER: 1G; PROTEIN: 1G; SODIUM: 30MG

VARIATION TIP: Add parsley, cilantro, or harissa (page 143) to add different flavors to this sauce. Tarator sauce is tahini sauce mixed with finely chopped fresh parsley. This sauce is popular drizzled over grilled fish or roasted vegetables.

BASIL PESTO

30 MINUTES OR LESS ✦ FREEZER FRIENDLY ✦ GLUTEN FREE

PREP TIME: 15 MINUTES • MAKES 1 CUP

Basil pesto is a sauce originating in Genoa, around the 16th century. Since then, it has been developed and regionally modified. Each person and family has their own spin on what makes their basil pesto the best. My secrets are in the preparation. At the end of summer, I pick all my basil and purée it with olive oil and a little salt, which I freeze in small packets. In this way, anytime during winter, if I need basil for pasta sauce, pizza, or pesto, I thaw a pack and can taste summer again.

2 cups packed chopped fresh basil

3 garlic cloves, peeled

¼ cup pine nuts

½ cup olive oil

½ teaspoon salt

½ cup freshly grated Parmesan cheese

1. In a food processor or blender, combine the basil, garlic, and pine nuts. Pulse until coarsely chopped.
2. Add the olive oil, salt, and Parmesan cheese. Process for 5 minutes until you have a smooth paste.
3. Refrigerate in an airtight container for up to 3 weeks, or freeze for up to 1 month.

PER SERVING: (1 TABLESPOON) CALORIES: 81; TOTAL FAT: 9G; SATURATED FAT: 2G; CARBOHYDRATES: 1G; FIBER: 0G; PROTEIN: 2G; SODIUM: 91MG

VARIATION TIP: Use fresh cilantro with pecans and walnut oil for a unique pesto to drizzle over grilled vegetables or roasted potatoes.

GARLIC AIOLI

30 MINUTES OR LESS ✦ DAIRY FREE ✦ GLUTEN FREE ✦ NUT FREE

PREP TIME: 15 MINUTES • MAKES 1 CUP

There are several versions of aioli. All start with a lot of mashed garlic, which is a favorite ingredient of Mediterranean cuisine. Basic aioli contains egg yolk, whereas other versions contain yogurt as an emulsifier, or cornstarch to bond the garlic and oil.

3 garlic cloves, minced

½ teaspoon salt

1 large egg yolk, at room temperature

1 cup olive oil

1. In a food processor, combine the garlic, salt, and egg yolk. Process for 1 minute.
2. While the food processor is running, slowly add the olive oil, drop by drop, until the oil is totally incorporated and you have a smooth mayonnaise-like paste.
3. Refrigerate in an airtight container for up to 1 week.

PER SERVING: (1 TABLESPOON) CALORIES: 112; TOTAL FAT: 13G; SATURATED FAT: 2G; CARBOHYDRATES: 0G; FIBER: 0G; PROTEIN: 0G; SODIUM: 74MG

PREP TIP: Make this aioli by hand: In a medium bowl, mash the garlic and salt into a smooth paste. Add the egg yolk and, using a fork or small whisk, whisk while slowly adding the oil drop by drop until incorporated.

HARISSA

30 MINUTES OR LESS ✦ GLUTEN FREE ✦ NUT FREE ✦ VEGAN

PREP TIME: 15 MINUTES • COOK TIME: 15 MINUTES • MAKES 1 CUP

I use this paste to make a spicy hummus, add a touch of warmth to a stew, and make an eye-catching and delicious red aioli. Harissa is traditionally made by drying seeded peppers on the roof or balcony for a couple days and then puréeing them with olive oil and salt. You can find mild, spicy, and extra-hot versions in any Mediterranean kitchen. The level of the spiciness comes from the variety of pepper used. In Syria, they use Aleppo pepper to make hot harissa. To achieve almost the same level of heat, I use red bell pepper for color and habaneros for the heat. Make sure to wear gloves when you seed the peppers and do not put your hands to your face.

½ cup olive oil, plus more as needed

1 red bell pepper, seeded and chopped

5 habanero peppers, seeded and chopped

2 tablespoons freshly squeezed lemon juice

1 tablespoon tomato paste

1 tablespoon ground cumin

1 teaspoon ground coriander

1 teaspoon paprika

½ teaspoon salt

1. In a sauté pan or skillet over medium heat, heat the olive oil.
2. Add the red bell pepper and habaneros and cook for 10 minutes.
3. Stir in the lemon juice, tomato paste, cumin, coriander, paprika, and salt until thoroughly combined. Cook for 2 to 3 minutes more.
4. Transfer the ingredients to a food processor or blender. Blend into a smooth paste. If the paste seems dry, add olive oil, 1 tablespoon at a time, until you reach your desired consistency.
5. Refrigerate in an airtight container for up to 2 months.

PER SERVING: (1 TABLESPOON) CALORIES: 65; TOTAL FAT: 7G; SATURATED FAT: 1G; CARBOHYDRATES: 2G; FIBER: 1G; PROTEIN: 1G; SODIUM: 77MG

TZATZIKI SAUCE

30 MINUTES OR LESS ✦ GLUTEN FREE ✦ NUT FREE

PREP TIME: 15 MINUTES • MAKES 2 CUPS

This yogurt sauce started on the Greek island of Paros. It is traditionally served with a kebab of grilled vegetables. The cooling combination of mint and yogurt makes it a great dip or topping for dishes with a bit of spice, or for something rich and hearty like my Brown Lentils and Bulgur with Crispy Onions (page 110).

2 garlic cloves, minced

1 teaspoon dried mint flakes (see tip)

½ teaspoon salt

2 cups Plain Yogurt (page 150), or store-bought

½ cup cold water

2 Persian cucumbers, chopped (optional)

1. In a medium bowl, stir together the garlic, mint, and salt.
2. Whisk in the yogurt and cold water until you have a smooth paste.
3. Stir in the cucumbers (if using). Chill before serving. Keep refrigerated in an airtight container for up to 1 week.

PER SERVING: (¼ CUP) CALORIES: 45; TOTAL FAT: 1G; SATURATED FAT: 1G; CARBOHYDRATES: 5G; FIBER: 0G; PROTEIN: 4G; SODIUM: 160MG

VARIATION TIP: This recipe also works well with dill, parsley, or thyme, depending on the flavor profile you want. You can also swap the dried herbs for 1 tablespoon chopped fresh herbs.

BASIC TOMATO BASIL SAUCE

30 MINUTES OR LESS ✦ GLUTEN FREE ✦ NUT FREE ✦ VEGAN

PREP TIME: 10 MINUTES • COOK TIME: 20 MINUTES • MAKES 4 CUPS

This is a staple in my home, and it's my go-to dish for lunch on a busy day. I typically spread it on Pita Bread (page 152) and sprinkle it with cheese for a quick healthy pizza. Sometimes I'll just bring it to a boil and drop in some broken angel hair pasta for a fast-and-easy tomato soup.

¼ cup olive oil

4 garlic cloves, crushed

1 (28-ounce) can crushed tomatoes

1 cup water

⅛ teaspoon salt

⅛ teaspoon freshly ground black pepper

1 cup chopped fresh basil

1. In a medium saucepan over medium heat, heat the olive oil.
2. Add the garlic and sear for 30 seconds.
3. Stir in the tomatoes, water, salt, and pepper. Bring to a boil, cover the pan, and simmer for 15 minutes, stirring occasionally.
4. Stir in the basil and cook for 2 to 3 minutes more. Refrigerate leftovers, cooled, in an airtight container for up to 1 week, or freeze for up to 6 weeks.

PER SERVING: (½ CUP) CALORIES: 88; TOTAL FAT: 7G; SATURATED FAT: 1G; CARBOHYDRATES: 8G; FIBER: 2G; PROTEIN: 2G; SODIUM: 165MG

BÉCHAMEL SAUCE

30 MINUTES OR LESS ✦ NUT FREE

PREP TIME: 10 MINUTES • COOK TIME: 15 MINUTES • MAKES 2 CUPS

Even though béchamel sauce is associated with French cooking, it was first made in Tuscany, Italy. It is purportedly named after Marquis Louis de Béchamel who, legend has it, needed something to moisten his lunch of dried cod. This rich and decadent sauce is a component of my Three Sauces Lasagna (page 125) and can be used in Eggplant Moussaka (page 86), too. In this recipe I use whole milk for richness, but if you want something a little lighter, I've created this sauce with 2-percent milk with delicious results.

2 cups whole milk

1 tablespoon butter

2 tablespoons
  all-purpose flour

¼ cup freshly grated
  Parmesan cheese

⅛ teaspoon freshly
  grated nutmeg

1. In a medium saucepan over low heat, heat the milk for 2 to 3 minutes. Turn off the heat but keep the pan on the burner to keep the milk warm.

2. In another medium saucepan over medium heat, melt the butter. Add the flour and cook for about 2 minutes, whisking continuously, until a smooth golden paste forms.

3. Add ¼ cup of warm milk to the flour paste and whisk to blend. Continue to cook over medium heat for about 10 minutes, slowly whisking in the warmed milk until the sauce thickens. Remove from the heat. Whisk in the Parmesan cheese and nutmeg until well combined.

PER SERVING: (¼ CUP) CALORIES: 68; TOTAL FAT: 4G; SATURATED FAT: 3G; CARBOHYDRATES: 4G; FIBER: 0G; PROTEIN: 3G; SODIUM: 67MG

SUBSTITUTION TIP: Skip the flour for a gluten-free sauce. Instead, mix 2 teaspoons cornstarch with ¼ cup cold water and add the slurry to the hot milk. Cook over medium heat until the sauce thickens.

PRESERVED LEMONS

GLUTEN FREE ✦ NUT FREE ✦ VEGAN

PREP TIME: 10 MINUTES • COOK TIME: 5 MINUTES
PRESERVING TIME: 1 MONTH, 3 DAYS

Preserved lemons add texture and a unique flavor to stews and tagines. Typically, Meyer lemons are used, but use any lemons you have on hand. When a recipe calls for preserved lemon, remove one from the jar, rinse off the salt, chop, and use.

5 lemons

2 tablespoons salt, divided

Freshly squeezed lemon juice, as needed

1. Bring a large saucepan filled three-fourths full with water to a boil over high heat. Add the lemons, reduce the heat to medium, and boil for 2 minutes. Remove from the heat and let cool. Drain.

2. Spoon 1 tablespoon of salt into a large (1-pint) Mason jar.

3. Cut off ½ inch from the top of each lemon and quarter the lemons from the top to within ½ inch of the bottom. Sprinkle the flesh of each lemon with about ½ teaspoon of salt. Close the lemon and push it into the jar. Repeat.

4. Use a wooden spoon to press the lemons to release their juices. If the juice released from the fruit does not cover them, add freshly squeezed lemon juice to cover. It's important that the lemons are submerged. Seal the jar tightly and let it stand at room temperature for 3 days, shaking the jar a few times each day.

5. After 3 days, place the jar in the refrigerator and let sit for 1 month before using. The preserved lemons will keep, sealed in the jar, for up to 1 year.

GHEE

30 MINUTES OR LESS ✦ GLUTEN FREE ✦ NUT FREE

PREP TIME: 5 MINUTES • COOK TIME: 20 MINUTES • MAKES 2 CUPS

Though this recipe originated in India, it came to the Mediterranean through trade with Turkey, quickly becoming an essential ingredient in the Eastern Mediterranean kitchen. Ghee, known as clarified butter, is typically made from cow's milk. When the butter is cooked with salt, the butter separates into liquid fats and the milk solids are trapped in the salt. Ghee can be a way for those with slight dairy sensitivity to enjoy the flavor of butter.

1 pound (4 sticks) unsalted
  butter, cut into 3-inch cubes

1 tablespoon salt

1. Place the butter in a large heavy-bottomed saucepan. This will promote even melting and prevent the butter from burning. Turn the heat to medium-low and simmer the butter for about 5 minutes until the milk solids float to the top. Skim off and discard the solids until all the floaters have been removed.

2. Continue to cook for about 10 minutes more or until the milk solids sink to the bottom and the butter turns clear. You now have clarified butter.

3. Continue cooking for about 5 minutes more or until the milk solids on the bottom of the pan turn light brown and the clarified butter becomes fragrant. You now have ghee. Make sure to pay attention to the butter as this change can happen quickly.

4. Let the ghee cool for 3 to 5 minutes. Carefully pour the golden liquid into a clean jar with a tight-fitting lid. Some people strain this liquid to remove any lingering solids, but it is not necessary. Ghee can be kept in a jar on a pantry shelf for up to 1 year with no need for refrigeration.

VARIATION TIP: Add a dash of ground cardamom for extra flavor.

PER SERVING: (1 TABLESPOON) CALORIES: 135; TOTAL FAT: 15G; SATURATED FAT: 9G; CARBOHYDRATES: 0G; FIBER: 0G; PROTEIN: 0G; SODIUM: 215MG

HERB-FLAVORED BUTTER

30 MINUTES OR LESS ✦ FREEZER FRIENDLY ✦ GLUTEN FREE ✦ NUT FREE

PREP TIME: 15 MINUTES • MAKES 1 CUP

Consider this butter an anytime treat. Spread it on toasted bread, drizzle it over roasted vegetables, or toss it with hot pasta for a deliciously simple dish. You can also spoon the butter onto wax paper and form it into a log. Refrigerate until firm and serve the log with your favorite bread.

½ cup finely chopped fresh basil, thyme, or cilantro

1 garlic clove, mashed

1 tablespoon freshly squeezed lemon juice

8 tablespoons (1 stick) unsalted butter, at room temperature

½ teaspoon white pepper

¼ teaspoon salt

Grated zest of 1 lemon

1. In a food processor, combine the basil, garlic, and lemon juice. Process until a smooth paste forms.
2. Add the butter, white pepper, salt, and lemon zest. Process until smooth and well mixed.
3. Spoon the butter into an airtight container and refrigerate until firm. The butter will keep, refrigerated in an airtight container, for up to 2 months, or frozen for up to 6 months.
4. To freeze it, wrap the butter tightly in wax paper. Remove from the freezer and thaw in the refrigerator for 24 hours before using.

PER SERVING: (1 TABLESPOON) CALORIES: 52; TOTAL FAT: 6G; SATURATED FAT: 4G; CARBOHYDRATES: 0G; FIBER: 0G; PROTEIN: 0G; SODIUM: 72MG

VARIATION TIP: Flavor the butter with fruit for a sweeter spread option. Stir together ½ cup butter, at room temperature, with ¼ cup of your favorite jam.

PLAIN YOGURT

GLUTEN FREE ✦ NUT FREE

PREP TIME: 15 MINUTES • COOK TIME: 30 MINUTES
FERMENTING TIME: 1 DAY • MAKES 5 CUPS

In Eastern Mediterranean countries, you can find yogurt shops just as you would find wine shops in the West. You'll find different varieties of yogurt made from cow's milk, sheep's milk, and goat's milk. My *sito*, grandmother, used to make smoked yogurt; she intentionally burned the milk while boiling it. My mom would cover the container of hot milk mixture with a winter coat and place it in a large box to maintain the warm temperature. You'll need a digital thermometer to make sure the milk is at the right temperature.

6 cups 2% milk, or whole milk

¼ cup plain yogurt (see tip)

INGREDIENT TIP: Plain yogurt used for yogurt making is sometimes called a "starter." After you make your first batch of yogurt, save 1 cup as the starter for your next batch and so on.

1. In a heavy-bottomed pot over medium heat, heat the milk until it begins to bubble at the edges and reaches 180°F, using a food thermometer to check the temperature. Stir the milk occasionally as it heats.
2. Carefully pour the hot milk into a large glass or stainless steel bowl. Let it sit off the heat for about 10 minutes or until it cools to 120°F.
3. In a small bowl, whisk the yogurt. Spoon it into the warm milk and stir to combine. Move the milk to a warm place. I use my oven with the light on. Let sit for at least 8 hours or up to 12 hours. It will get thicker and tangier the longer it sits.
4. Remove the bowl from its resting place and refrigerate the yogurt until cold, about 8 hours. It will continue to thicken as it chills.

PER SERVING: (½ CUP) CALORIES: 78; TOTAL FAT: 3G; SATURATED FAT: 2G; CARBOHYDRATES: 8G; FIBER: 0G; PROTEIN: 5G; SODIUM: 73MG

ORANGE BLOSSOM SYRUP

30 MINUTES OR LESS ✦ GLUTEN FREE ✦ NUT FREE ✦ VEGAN

PREP TIME: 5 MINUTES • COOK TIME: 15 MINUTES • MAKES 2 CUPS

Traditionally, honey was used as the syrup for baklava and other Mediterranean desserts, but as the price of honey rose and people could no longer afford it, orange blossom syrup became the go-to substitution. The delicately flavored orange blossom water is made from the essential oil of orange blossoms, which is readily available online or can be found in the Middle Eastern section of your grocery store. I think it's worth the effort to find it. Once opened, it will last for up to 1 year.

2 cups sugar

1½ cups water

1 tablespoon freshly squeezed lemon juice

1 tablespoon orange blossom water (see tip)

1. In a small saucepan over medium heat, stir together the sugar, water, and lemon juice. Bring to a boil. Reduce the heat to medium and cook the syrup for 15 minutes.
2. Remove from the heat, stir in the orange blossom water, and let cool before using. Refrigerate in an airtight container for up to 1 month.

PER SERVING: (1 TABLESPOON) CALORIES: 47; TOTAL FAT: 0G; SATURATED FAT: 0G; CARBOHYDRATES: 13G; FIBER: 0G; PROTEIN: 0G; SODIUM: 0MG

SUBSTITUTION TIP: Use vanilla as a flavoring agent instead of orange blossom water in the same amount.

PITA BREAD

FREEZER FRIENDLY ✦ NUT FREE ✦ VEGAN

PREP TIME: 20 MINUTES • REST TIME: 1 HOUR, 10 MINUTES
COOK TIME: 20 MINUTES • MAKES 8 LOAVES

You can use this dough to make Cheese and Parsley Flatbread (page 132), Flatbread with Harissa and Sesame (page 133), or create pita pizzas with your favorite toppings.

1 tablespoon active dry yeast

1 tablespoon sugar

1½ cups water, divided

2½ cups all-purpose flour, plus more for dusting, divided

1 teaspoon salt

1 tablespoon olive oil

FREEZING TIP: You can freeze the dough: Moisten your palms with olive oil and cut the dough into 8 balls. Place the balls on a baking sheet and freeze overnight. Transfer the frozen dough balls to a freezer-safe bag and keep frozen for up to 2 months. When ready to use, remove one or two balls and allow the dough to thaw in the refrigerator overnight before baking as directed.

1. In a cup, stir together the yeast, sugar, and ½ cup of warm water. Let sit for about 5 minutes for the yeast to activate.

2. In a medium bowl, whisk 2 cups of flour and the salt to combine. Add the yeast mixture and mix. While mixing, 1 tablespoon at a time, add the remaining ½ cup of warm water until the flour is mixed thoroughly and a dough forms.

3. Dust your hands and a work surface with flour. Turn the dough out on to the flour and knead it for about 5 minutes or until smooth. If needed, dust your palms with more flour to prevent the dough from sticking to your hands.

4. Coat another medium bowl with the olive oil and transfer the dough to the prepared bowl. Cover the dough and let rest for 1 hour.

5. Preheat the oven to 500°F.

6. Divide the dough into 8 (3-inch) balls. Cover them with a clean kitchen towel and let rest for 10 minutes.

7. Dust a work surface with flour. Roll each ball into a ⅛-inch-thick round and let them rest for 5 minutes. Place 2 rounds on a baking sheet.

8. Bake for 3 to 5 minutes until the bread puffs up. Remove from the oven and repeat with the remaining dough rounds.

PER SERVING: (1 LOAF) CALORIES: 155; TOTAL FAT: 2G; SATURATED FAT: 0G; CARBOHYDRATES: 30G; FIBER: 2G; PROTEIN: 5G; SODIUM: 293MG

PIZZA DOUGH

30 MINUTES OR LESS ✦ FREEZER FRIENDLY ✦ VEGAN

PREP TIME: 30 MINUTES • MAKES 2 (14-INCH) PIZZAS

Pizza dough has many uses beyond the traditional Margherita Pizza (page 130). Use it to make Spinach and Walnut Fatayers (page 27), Rosemary Focaccia (page 134), or Spiced Lentils with Dumplings (page 116). This recipe yields about 2 pounds of dough.

3 cups bread flour, plus more as needed

1 teaspoon sugar

2 teaspoons salt

1 (0.25-ounce) packet instant dry yeast

1½ cups warm water, plus more as needed

¼ cup olive oil, divided

1. In the bowl of a stand mixer fitted with the dough hook attachment, combine the flour, sugar, salt, and yeast.
2. Start mixing at low speed while slowly adding the warm water and 2 tablespoons of olive oil. Keep mixing at low to medium speed until the dough forms into a ball. Add 2 tablespoons more water if the dough is dry, or sprinkle it with a couple tablespoons of flour if the dough is sticky. The dough should be smooth.
3. Coat a medium bowl with the remaining 2 tablespoons of olive oil. Place the dough in the prepared bowl and knead it into a smooth but firm ball. Use directly, or refrigerate the dough, covered, for up to 2 days. The dough will expand. Punch it down when you take it out of the refrigerator and let it come to room temperature before you flatten it for your pizza.

PER SERVING: (¼ PIZZA CRUST) CALORIES: 229; TOTAL FAT: 7G; SATURATED FAT: 1G; CARBOHYDRATES: 36G; FIBER: 6G; PROTEIN: 6G; SODIUM: 0MG

FREEZING TIP: Divide the dough into 2 balls, moisten with olive oil, wrap in plastic wrap, and freeze for up to 3 months. When ready to use, thaw the wrapped pizza dough ball in the refrigerator overnight. Place it on the counter to warm to room temperature about 30 minutes before proceeding.

VARIATION TIP: Use all-purpose flour for a chewier crust.

HOMEMADE FALAFEL MIX

FREEZER FRIENDLY ✦ GLUTEN FREE ✦ NUT FREE ✦ VEGAN

SOAK TIME: 24 HOURS • PREP TIME: 15 MINUTES • DRAIN TIME: 30 MINUTES
MAKES 40 SMALL PATTIES

This fragrant mixture of ground chickpeas and herbs is formed into patties and deep-fried or baked. They can be eaten as part of a Falafel Sandwich (page 52) or placed over greens for a filling salad. Falafel works with almost any toppings. Tahini Sauce (page 140), Hummus (page 10), and Pickled Turnips (page 19) are some of my favorites, but experiment to find your favorite combination. I always keep some of this mix on hand for an easy snack or quick dinner option.

1 pound dried chickpeas

1 large onion, chopped

2 cups chopped fresh parsley

½ cup chopped fresh cilantro

2 garlic cloves, mashed, or
 ¼ teaspoon garlic powder

1 tablespoon ground coriander

1 tablespoon ground cumin

1 teaspoon salt

1 tablespoon baking powder

1. In a large bowl, combine the chickpeas with enough cold water to cover. Let soak for 24 hours. Drain the chickpeas and transfer to a medium bowl.
2. Add the onion, parsley, and cilantro and mix well. A spoonful at a time, transfer the mixture to a food processor or blender and process in batches until you have a thick paste.
3. Spoon the paste into a colander and allow any liquid to drain for 30 minutes. Transfer the chickpea paste to a large bowl.
4. Stir in the garlic, coriander, cumin, salt, and baking powder. Use directly, or refrigerate in an airtight container for up to 5 days.

PER SERVING: (4 PATTIES) CALORIES: 180; TOTAL FAT: 3G; SATURATED FAT: 0G; CARBOHYDRATES: 31G; FIBER: 9G; PROTEIN: 10G; SODIUM: 254MG

MAKE AHEAD: You can freeze this falafel mixture for 6 months. Freeze it at the end of step 3. You want to add fresh spices before frying or baking. Spoon the falafel into a freezer bag; massage the bag to get out all the air, seal, and freeze. When ready to use, thaw, let come to room temperature, and add the spices to fry.

CHAPTER 8
SWEETS AND DESSERTS

RED WINE-POACHED PEARS

GLUTEN FREE ✦ NUT FREE ✦ VEGAN

PREP TIME: 5 MINUTES • COOK TIME: 35 MINUTES • SERVES 4

This classic French dessert is one of my favorite ways to add a touch of elegance to a dinner party. Despite being super simple to prepare, these pears never fail to impress guests. The red wine produces a beautiful deep red color and is a great way to use up the open bottle you might have on hand. I suggest serving the pears with a side of vanilla ice cream or mascarpone cheese if you want to cut the sweetness a bit, though note that the recipe will no longer be vegan.

4 cups dry red wine, or cranberry juice

1 cup sugar

½ cup dried cranberries

Grated zest of 1 lemon

4 Bosc pears, peeled with stems intact

1. In a large saucepan over medium heat, combine the red wine, sugar, cranberries, and lemon zest. Bring to a boil.
2. Using tongs, gently lower the pears into the boiling mixture. Reduce the heat to low, cover the pan, and simmer for 20 minutes, turning the pears every 5 minutes.
3. Remove the pears from the cooking liquid and place on a platter. Set aside.
4. Reduce the heat to low and continue to cook the liquid for 5 to 10 minutes more until it is slightly syrupy. Drizzle the liquid over the pears and let the pears cool slightly before serving.
5. Slice the pears in half, if desired, and drizzle with the syrup. Let them cool slightly before serving.

PER SERVING: CALORIES: 335; TOTAL FAT: 1G; SATURATED FAT: 0G; CARBOHYDRATES: 71G; FIBER: 7G; PROTEIN: 1G; SODIUM: 8MG

VARIATION TIP: Use white wine and cinnamon sticks in place of the red wine and cranberries for a different flavor profile.

CLASSIC RICE PUDDING

GLUTEN FREE

PREP TIME: 10 MINUTES • COOK TIME: 1 HOUR, 20 MINUTES • SERVES 6

You will find this *rizogal*, which means "rice milk," in Greek milk and yogurt shops. You can serve this pudding hot or cold, with or with toasted almonds—whatever way you choose is sure to be delicious!

4 cups 2% milk

¾ cup sugar

2 whole cloves

2 cinnamon sticks

6 cups water

½ cup short-grain rice

2 large eggs

¼ teaspoon ground cinnamon

¼ cup chopped toasted almonds (optional)

1. In a heavy-bottomed saucepan over medium heat, stir together the milk and sugar. Add the cloves and cinnamon sticks. Cook for about 15 minutes until the milk begins to bubble along the edges but does not boil. Turn off the heat. Let sit for 10 minutes. Set aside.
2. In a medium saucepan over medium heat, combine the water and rice. Cook for about 15 minutes until the rice is cooked but not mushy. Drain the rice and add it to the cooked, cooled milk.
3. Return the saucepan with the milk-and-rice mixture to medium heat. Cook, stirring often, for about 30 minutes until thickened. Remove from the heat and remove and discard the cloves and cinnamon sticks. Set aside.
4. In a small bowl, whisk the eggs until frothy. Whisk in about ½ cup of the milk-and-rice mixture and mix well. Pour this back into the saucepan.
5. Return the saucepan to medium heat. Cook, stirring constantly, for about 5 minutes.
6. Spoon the pudding into custard cups, dust with the cinnamon, and top with the toasted almonds (if using).

PER SERVING: CALORIES: 276; TOTAL FAT: 7G; SATURATED FAT: 3G; CARBOHYDRATES: 46G; FIBER: 1G; PROTEIN: 9G; SODIUM: 98MG

MILK AND ORANGE PUDDING

GLUTEN FREE

PREP TIME: 10 MINUTES • COOK TIME: 20 MINUTES
CHILL TIME: 1 HOUR, 10 MINUTES PLUS OVERNIGHT • SERVES 4

This eye-catching multilayered dessert is light and refreshing on a hot summer's night. The combination of silky smooth pudding and crunchy pistachios is a delight. It's also high in protein, calcium, vitamin C, and other nutrients, but you don't need to tell your guests that—they'll be too distracted by how delicious it is to wonder whether it's good for them. You can use vanilla extract in place of orange blossom water, but I highly recommend trying it this way, if you can.

FOR THE MILK PUDDING

3 tablespoons cornstarch

¼ cup cold water

4 cups 2% milk

1 cup sugar

1 tablespoon orange
   blossom water

FOR THE ORANGE PUDDING

1 tablespoon cornstarch

¼ cup cold water

1½ cups freshly squeezed
   orange juice

1 tablespoon orange
   blossom water

4 tablespoons crushed
   unsalted pistachios

TO MAKE THE MILK PUDDING

1. In a small bowl, stir together the cornstarch and cold water until the cornstarch dissolves.
2. In a medium saucepan over medium heat, stir together the milk and sugar.
3. Add the cornstarch mixture. Cook, stirring constantly, for about 15 minutes until the mixture thickens and it coats the spoon.
4. Turn off the heat, stir in the orange blossom water, and spoon evenly into 4 sundae or parfait dishes. Leave at least 1 inch at the top for the orange pudding.
5. Let the milk pudding cool at room temperature for 1 hour before making the orange pudding.

TO MAKE THE ORANGE PUDDING

1. In a small bowl, stir together the cornstarch and cold water until the cornstarch dissolves.
2. In a medium saucepan over medium heat, stir together the orange juice and cornstarch mixture.
3. Cook for about 5 minutes, stirring constantly, until the mixture thickens and it coats the back of a spoon.

4. Remove from the heat, stir in the orange blossom water, and let cool for 10 minutes.
5. Divide the orange pudding evenly among the parfait dishes with the milk pudding, and smooth out the top layer.
6. Sprinkle each serving with 1 tablespoon of pistachios. Refrigerate overnight before serving.

PER SERVING: CALORIES: 399; TOTAL FAT: 6G; SATURATED FAT: 3G; CARBOHYDRATES: 81G; FIBER: 0G; PROTEIN: 9G; SODIUM: 101MG

VARIATION TIP: Use mango nectar instead of orange juice for a delicious tropical twist!

CRÈME CARAMEL

GLUTEN FREE ✦ NUT FREE

PREP TIME: 20 MINUTES • COOK TIME: 1 HOUR • CHILL TIME: 3 HOURS • SERVES 6

Crème caramel is a classic French dessert that you might also know as flan. Whatever you call it, it's hard to beat the velvety smooth texture and almost savory caramel sweetness.

1½ cups sugar, divided

½ cup water, plus more as needed

3 cups milk

4 large egg yolks

2 teaspoons vanilla extract

Grated zest of 1 orange

1. Preheat the oven to 325°F.
2. In a heavy-bottomed saucepan over low heat, combine 1 cup of sugar and the water. Cook until the sugar dissolves, carefully brushing the walls of the pot with a little water to prevent the sugar from crystallizing on the sides.
3. Increase the heat to medium-high and boil until a syrup forms and turns golden brown. Remove from the heat and carefully pour the syrup into 6 ramekins. Set aside to cool.
4. In a medium saucepan over medium heat, heat the milk until hot but not boiling.
5. In a medium bowl, whisk the egg yolks with the remaining ½ cup of sugar, vanilla, and orange zest. While whisking continually, slowly add the warmed milk to the egg mixture, whisking until well combined.
6. Using a fine-mesh sieve, strain the milk-and-egg mixture into a bowl. Pour the strained mixture into the ramekins. Place the ramekins in a large roasting pan and add enough water to come halfway up the sides of the ramekins.
7. Bake for about 35 minutes or until the custard is just set. Remove from the oven, carefully remove the ramekins from the hot water, and let cool for 15 minutes.
8. Cover and refrigerate for 3 hours before serving. To unmold, run a sharp knife around the inside of each ramekin and carefully invert onto a serving plate.

PER SERVING: CALORIES: 288; TOTAL FAT: 6G; SATURATED FAT: 3G; CARBOHYDRATES: 57G; FIBER: 0G; PROTEIN: 6G; SODIUM: 63MG

NO-BAKE SPICED FIG LOAF

GLUTEN FREE ✦ VEGAN

PREP TIME: 20 MINUTES • CHILL TIME: 48 HOURS • SERVES 8

The warm climate of Southern Spain is famous for producing large crops of figs, though most found in your local grocery store probably come from California. This candy-like dessert is one of my favorite ways to use figs and doesn't require you to turn on your oven or stove.

1½ pounds dried Mission figs, stemmed and finely chopped

1 cup almonds, toasted and finely chopped

½ cup orange marmalade

¼ cup granulated sugar

1 tablespoon olive oil, plus more for moistening

1 tablespoon aniseed

1 teaspoon ground cinnamon

¼ teaspoon ground nutmeg

Grated zest of 1 orange

1 tablespoon powdered sugar

1. In a food processor, combine the figs and almonds and pulse for 1 minute. Add the marmalade, granulated sugar, olive oil, aniseed, cinnamon, nutmeg, and orange zest. Pulse until well combined.

2. Spoon the mixture into a medium bowl, knead for 10 minutes, and shape into a large loaf.

3. Moisten a large piece of wax paper with a little olive oil and wrap the wax paper around the loaf. Refrigerate for 2 days before cutting and serving.

4. When ready to serve, dust with powdered sugar.

PER SERVING: CALORIES: 264; TOTAL FAT: 9G; SATURATED FAT: 1G; CARBOHYDRATES: 48G; FIBER: 6G; PROTEIN: 4G; SODIUM: 15MG

MAKE AHEAD: Wrap the loaf in plastic wrap and keep refrigerated for up to 3 months.

AFTER-DINNER PICK-ME-UPS

People living in the Mediterranean region are just as serious about their coffee as they are about their food. Most prefer it dark and strong, but sometimes they also like it sweet. Here are a couple of the easiest ways to enjoy your caffeine fix for dessert—or your dessert for breakfast.

Affogato: Popularized in Italy, *affogato*, which translates to "drowned," has quickly appeared on American coffee shop menus. It's a snap to make at home and is a surefire pick-me-up. Simply pour 1 shot of your favorite espresso (or an equal amount of strongly brewed coffee) over a scoop of your favorite gelato or ice cream. The bitterness of the coffee is tempered by the sweetness of the ice cream—and there's no need for cream or sugar!

Greek frappe: This frothy treat doesn't require you to brew any coffee and is perfect for hot summer days. In a container with a tight-fitting lid, combine 2 teaspoons of instant coffee (typically Nescafé), 1 teaspoon of sugar, and 1 tablespoon of water. Cover and shake vigorously for 30 seconds or until the contents are foamy. Pour the foam into an ice-filled glass and slowly top with cold water or milk until the glass is full. Use more or less sugar depending on your taste.

THE BEST BAKLAVA

PREP TIME: 40 MINUTES • COOK TIME: 50 MINUTES • REST TIME: OVERNIGHT • SERVES 12

There's nothing like the combination of sweetness, flaky filo dough, and crunchy walnuts that you get from baklava. The Eastern Mediterranean is full of different recipes for this classic dessert. Each country claims to make the best one, and every family has its own version. This is my family's version—which is the best, of course!

4 cups crushed walnuts

½ cup sugar

2 tablespoons ground cinnamon

1 cup melted Ghee (page 148) or butter, divided

24 sheets filo dough; follow the instructions on the package to prevent drying

4 cups Orange Blossom Syrup (page 151)

VARIATION TIP: For easy baklava, brush 6 filo sheets with melted butter, cut into 4-inch squares, and push the squares gently into muffin cups. Spoon 1 tablespoon of walnut mixture into each. Bake for 10 minutes in a 300°F oven and drizzle with the syrup to serve.

1. In a small bowl, stir together the walnuts, sugar, and cinnamon. Set aside.
2. Brush the bottom and sides of a 9-by-13-inch baking dish with some ghee. Place 2 sheets of filo in the dish and brush thoroughly with ghee. Top with 2 more filo sheets and brush with ghee. Repeat until you have used 12 sheets of filo dough.
3. Spread the walnut mixture evenly over the filo dough. Drizzle with 1 tablespoon of ghee.
4. Top with 2 sheets of filo dough, brush with ghee, and repeat until you have used the remaining filo dough. Brush the top layer with the remaining ghee. Refrigerate for 10 minutes.
5. Preheat the oven to 300°F.
6. Using a sharp knife, cut the baklava into diamond shapes.
7. Bake for 50 minutes or until the baklava is golden.
8. While the baklava is still hot, pour the orange blossom syrup over the top, making sure all the pastry is covered with the syrup. Let rest overnight before serving.

PER SERVING: CALORIES: 708; TOTAL FAT: 35G; SATURATED FAT: 12G; CARBOHYDRATES: 100G; FIBER: 3G; PROTEIN: 7G; SODIUM: 294MG

CINNAMON BISCOTTI

FREEZER FRIENDLY ✦ NUT FREE

PREP TIME: 20 MINUTES • COOK TIME: 55 MINUTES
COOL TIME: 2 HOURS, 20 MINUTES • MAKES 30 BISCOTTI

Biscotti are twice-baked hard cookies that can be stored for a long time and are perfect to dip into coffee and tea. They can come dipped in chocolate or studded with dried fruit, but I like the simplicity of this version.

2 cups all-purpose flour

3 teaspoons ground
cinnamon, divided

1 teaspoon baking powder

¼ teaspoon salt

1 cup sugar, divided

6 tablespoons unsalted butter,
at room temperature

3 large eggs

¼ cup freshly squeezed
orange juice

1 teaspoon vanilla extract

1. Preheat the oven to 325°F. Line a baking sheet with parchment paper.
2. In a medium bowl, whisk the flour, 2 teaspoons of cinnamon, the baking powder, and salt. Set aside.
3. In a large bowl, combine all but 2 tablespoons of sugar and the butter. Using a handheld electric mixer, beat until fluffy.
4. Add 2 eggs and beat well to combine. Mix in the orange juice and vanilla until blended.
5. Add the flour mixture to the butter mixture combine until a dough forms. Divide the dough in half. Shape each half into a 9-inch-long log. Transfer the logs to the prepared baking sheet.
6. In a small bowl, whisk the remaining egg. Brush the logs with the egg wash.
7. Bake for 40 minutes. Remove and let cool for 20 minutes. Leave the oven on.
8. In a small bowl, stir together the reserved 2 tablespoons of sugar and remaining 1 teaspoon of cinnamon.
9. Using a serrated knife, cut the logs at a 45-degree angle into ½-inch-thick slices. Place the biscotti, cut-side down, on a baking sheet. Dust with the cinnamon-sugar and bake for 15 minutes. Let cool for a couple hours before serving.

MAKE AHEAD: Wrap the logs and refrigerate for 1 week or freeze for 1 month. Thaw the frozen logs before baking.

PER SERVING: (2 COOKIES) CALORIES: 170; TOTAL FAT: 6G; SATURATED FAT: 3G; CARBOHYDRATES: 27G; FIBER: 1G; PROTEIN: 3G; SODIUM: 86MG

ORANGE AND ALMOND CAKE

DAIRY FREE ✦ GLUTEN FREE

PREP TIME: 15 MINUTES • COOK TIME: 45 MINUTES • REST TIME: 30 MINUTES • SERVES 8

When a friend or neighbor stops by in the Mediterranean, offering a tasty dessert is a must. It can be as simple as a bowl of fresh fruit or a plate of stuffed dates. The next time you have visitors, serve this recipe—and don't be surprised if they ask for seconds.

½ cup olive oil, plus more for preparing the cake pan

1 cup ground almonds

1½ cups sugar, divided

2 teaspoons baking powder

4 large eggs

Grated zest of 2 oranges

1 cup freshly squeezed orange juice

5 whole cloves

Grated zest of 1 lemon

¼ teaspoon ground cardamom

1. Preheat the oven to 350°F. Coat an 8-inch round cake pan with olive oil. Set aside.
2. In a medium bowl, stir together the almonds, 1 cup of sugar, and the baking powder.
3. In another medium bowl, whisk the eggs, olive oil, and orange zest. Add the egg mixture to the almond mixture. Whisk well to combine and spoon into the prepared cake pan.
4. Bake on the middle rack for 45 minutes or until the top is golden.
5. While the cake bakes, in a medium saucepan over medium heat, stir together the remaining ½ cup of sugar, orange juice, cloves, lemon zest, and cardamom. Bring to a boil, stirring occasionally, and cook for 5 to 8 minutes until the mixture is syrupy. Set aside.
6. Remove the cake from the oven. Drizzle it with the syrup and let it soak into the cake. Let the cake rest for 30 minutes before serving.

PER SERVING: CALORIES: 371; TOTAL FAT: 19G; SATURATED FAT: 3G; CARBOHYDRATES: 47G; FIBER: 1G; PROTEIN: 6G; SODIUM: 32MG

SERVING TIP: Sprinkle with toasted slivered almonds or chopped candied orange peel.

SEMOLINA AND SYRUP CAKE

PREP TIME: 15 MINUTES • COOK TIME: 40 MINUTES • COOL TIME: 2 HOURS • SERVES 12

Traditionally called *namoura*, this egg-free dessert derives its unique texture from the plain yogurt in the batter and the syrup it is soaked in before serving. The flavor combination of the semolina flour, orange blossom syrup, and tahini is perfect for serving with coffee or tea.

1 tablespoon tahini

3 cups semolina flour, or uncooked Cream of Wheat cereal

¾ cup Ghee (page 148), or store-bought, at room temperature

½ cup sugar

1 cup Plain Yogurt (page 150) plus 1 tablespoon, or store-bought

1½ teaspoons baking soda

12 almonds

2 cups Orange Blossom Syrup (page 151)

1. Preheat the oven to 400°F. Coat a 9-by-13-inch baking dish with the tahini.
2. In a medium bowl, stir together the semolina, ghee, and sugar. Set aside.
3. In a small bowl, whisk 1 cup of yogurt with the baking soda. Set aside for 5 minutes.
4. Add the yogurt mixture to the semolina mixture and mix well to combine. Spoon the batter into the prepared baking dish.
5. Moisten your palms with the remaining 1 tablespoon of yogurt and smooth the top of the cake. Lightly shake the pan to settle the batter. Lightly press a knife blade into the batter–do not cut all the way through—to mark 2-inch squares or diamond-shaped pieces. Place 1 almond in the center of each piece.
6. Bake for 40 minutes or until golden.
7. Pour the syrup over the warm cake and let it soak into the cake. Let cool for at least 2 hours before serving.

PER SERVING: CALORIES: 413; TOTAL FAT: 18G; SATURATED FAT: 10G; CARBOHYDRATES: 62G; FIBER: 1G; PROTEIN: 5G; SODIUM: 170MG

CLAFOUTIS

NUT FREE

PREP TIME: 10 MINUTES • COOK TIME: 30 MINUTES
COOL TIME: 10 MINUTES • SERVES 4 TO 6

This elegant French dessert is deceptively easy to make! A simple, egg-based batter is dotted with fruit and baked until golden. Traditionally made with cherries, it's a wonderfully delicious way to use a variety of fruits, including raspberries or blueberries, or even apples or pears, depending on the season.

3 tablespoons melted butter, at room temperature, plus more for preparing the pan

½ cup all-purpose flour

½ cup sugar

¼ teaspoon salt

3 large eggs

Grated zest of 2 lemons

⅓ cup whole milk

3 cups cherries, pitted

1 tablespoon powdered sugar, for serving

1. Preheat the oven to 350°F. Coat a 9-inch round baking pan with butter. Set aside.
2. In a medium bowl, whisk the flour, sugar, and salt. Set aside.
3. In another medium bowl, whisk the eggs. Add the lemon zest, melted butter, and milk. Whisk to combine. Pour the egg mixture over the flour mixture and whisk for about 3 minutes until very smooth.
4. Pour the batter into the prepared pan. Arrange the cherries on top.
5. Bake for 30 minutes or until the clafoutis is set and golden. Let cool for 10 minutes, and dust with the powdered sugar before serving.

PER SERVING: CALORIES: 188; TOTAL FAT: 7G; SATURATED FAT: 4G; CARBOHYDRATES: 28G; FIBER: 2G; PROTEIN: 4G; SODIUM: 135MG

THE DIRTY DOZEN™
AND CLEAN FIFTEEN™

A nonprofit environmental watchdog organization called Environmental Working Group (EWG) looks at data about pesticide residues supplied by the United States Department of Agriculture (USDA) and the Food and Drug Administration (FDA). Each year it compiles a list of the best and worst pesticide loads found in commercial crops. You can use these lists to decide which fruits and vegetables to buy organic to minimize your exposure to pesticides and which produce is considered safe enough to buy conventionally. This does not mean they are pesticide-free, though, so wash these fruits and vegetables thoroughly. The list is updated annually, and you can find it online at EWG.org/FoodNews.

Dirty Dozen™

1. strawberries
2. spinach
3. kale
4. nectarines
5. apples
6. grapes
7. peaches
8. cherries
9. pears
10. tomatoes
11. celery
12. potatoes

Additionally, nearly three-quarters of hot pepper samples contained pesticide residues.

Clean Fifteen™

1. avocados
2. sweet corn
3. pineapples
4. sweet peas (frozen)
5. onions
6. papayas
7. eggplants
8. asparagus
9. kiwis
10. cabbages
11. cauliflower
12. cantaloupes
13. broccoli
14. mushrooms
15. honeydew melons

MEASUREMENT CONVERSIONS

VOLUME EQUIVALENTS (LIQUID)

US STANDARD	US STANDARD (OUNCES)	METRIC (APPROXIMATE)
2 tablespoons	1 fl. oz.	30 mL
¼ cup	2 fl. oz.	60 mL
½ cup	4 fl. oz.	120 mL
1 cup	8 fl. oz.	240 mL
1½ cups	12 fl. oz.	355 mL
2 cups or 1 pint	16 fl. oz.	475 mL
4 cups or 1 quart	32 fl. oz.	1 L
1 gallon	128 fl. oz.	4 L

OVEN TEMPERATURES

FAHRENHEIT (F)	CELSIUS (C) (APPROXIMATE)
250°	120°
300°	150°
325°	165°
350°	180°
375°	190°
400°	200°
425°	220°
450°	230°

VOLUME EQUIVALENTS (DRY)

US STANDARD	METRIC (APPROXIMATE)
⅛ teaspoon	0.5 mL
¼ teaspoon	1 mL
½ teaspoon	2 mL
¾ teaspoon	4 mL
1 teaspoon	5 mL
1 tablespoon	15 mL
¼ cup	59 mL
⅓ cup	79 mL
½ cup	118 mL
⅔ cup	156 mL
¾ cup	177 mL
1 cup	235 mL
2 cups or 1 pint	475 mL
3 cups	700 mL
4 cups or 1 quart	1 L

WEIGHT EQUIVALENTS

US STANDARD	METRIC (APPROXIMATE)
½ ounce	15 g
1 ounce	30 g
2 ounces	60 g
4 ounces	115 g
8 ounces	225 g
12 ounces	340 g
16 ounces or 1 pound	455 g

INDEX

ABOUT THE AUTHOR

SANAA ABOUREZK was born and raised in Damascus, Syria. She received her bachelor of science degree in agricultural engineering from Damascus University and came to the United States to pursue her masters in food and nutrition from California State Polytechnic University, Pomona.

She attended Le Cordon Bleu culinary school in Paris to improve her baking skills as well as the Masha Innocenti cooking school in Florence, Italy, to learn the Italian art of sauces. Sanaa believes her academic education and culinary training have complemented each other to provide a comprehensive understanding of food—from its cultivation and role within the body to making cooking and eating an enjoyable experience.

Sanaa has published four cookbooks and, in 2003, opened her popular Mediterranean restaurant, Sanaa's Gourmet, in Sioux Falls, South Dakota. The restaurant has received numerous accolades including being named one of the top vegetarian restaurants in the United States in 2018 by Food Network's online magazine, and coverage by the *New York Times*. In addition, Sanaa was featured on the 2016 season finale of Food Network's *Beat Bobby Flay* and attended the James Beard Chef Boot Camp in 2018.

Sanaa believes in not only providing healthy gourmet meals at an affordable price, but also in giving back to the community. Each year, Sanaa hosts an annual charity dinner where 100 percent of the proceeds are donated to Feeding South Dakota. In addition, she also hosts numerous fundraisers for the Hungry Hearts of South Dakota.

Sanaa continues to reside in Sioux Falls, South Dakota, and her favorite time to cook is with her daughter, Alya, whenever she is home from college.

Printed in the USA
CPSIA information can be obtained
at www.ICGtesting.com
CBHW081247200224
4497CB00002B/8